Life Lessons of a Prodigal Son

A True Story of
Dreams from God

Moses Elijah

GOD BLESS YOU!

Publisher's Note. This publication is designed to provide accurate and authoritative information in regard to the subject matter. It is sold with the understanding that the publisher is not engaged in rendering professional career, legal, financial, psychological or health services. If expert assistance is required, the service of the appropriate professional should be sought.

Edited by Clarence Z. Seacrest

Cover design by Graphic_Pro247 and maxphotomaster

ISBN 978-0-9994790-4-9 (paperback)

ISBN 978-0-9994790-5-6 (ebook)

ISBN 978-0-9994790-6-3 (ebook)

Dedication

To my loving Father God who made the Way back home for me.

To my loving Lord Jesus Christ who became the Way home for me.

To my loving Holy Spirit who showed me the Way home.

Table of Contents

Introduction

Though a righteous man falls seven times, he will get up, but the wicked will stumble into ruin.
Proverbs 24:16 HCSB

Have you ever had a nightmare while sleeping? Have you ever had a nightmare that repeated itself each night for several nights? Have you ever had any dream that left you with a strong premonition, whether it was pleasant or a nightmare, which came true in your life?

What I'm about to tell you is a true story. Actually, it's a true story about multiple recurring dreams that came true in a person's life. No, I'm not talking about the dream Joseph had that came true in his life, making him a ruler in Egypt (Genesis 37:5); or the dream pharaoh of Egypt had that Joseph interpreted and came true (Genesis 41:1); or the dream that King Nebuchadnezzar of Babylon had that the prophet Daniel interpreted and came true (Daniel 2:1). This dream that came true was dreamed multiple times by a person who is alive today in your lifetime. That person has been living that dream all their life—over and over again.

Like so many other dreams that God gave people in the Bible, these dreams were not meant just for the person who dreamt them but also for the people who heard about the dream. So it is with this dream I'm about to share with you because it is a message for *you* today.

I'm that person who had those dreams and then lived them out in my life. I dreamt the same dream nightmare over and over again each night for 7 nights in a row. The real nightmare though was not just the dream itself but the fact that the dream came true in my life over and over again. And the message in this dream is about to come true in your life too, if it hasn't already started to happen.

What I'm about to share with you is not a coincidence of occurrences or circumstances that somehow magically happened to line up with events in my life over time throughout the course of my life. It was God's way of speaking to me in a dream; multiple recurring dreams in fact to tell me what was going to happen in my future. God was making a clear, strong statement to me in those recurring dreams the same way He was making a clear, strong statement to Joseph, pharaoh of Egypt and King Nebuchadnezzar when God gave them multiple dreams about what was about to happen in their future.

Of course, dreams aren't the only way God speaks to people. He can speak to us audibly (1 Samuel 3:4–10); in our spirit directly through His Holy Spirit (John 14:26); or through His written word in the Bible (Hebrews 4:12) or through other books such as this book you're reading (John 21:25). He speaks to us through people (2 Timothy 3:16) such as family, friends, strangers, angels (Daniel 10:12), co-workers, pastors and prophets (Matthew 23:33–37) or even through a donkey if He wants to (Numbers 22:28–30). He can speak to us in music, in nature (Psalm 19:1), in Christian broadcasting, and in visions and television. God's voice can be as loud as thunder (Job 37:2, Revelation 14:2, 2 Samuel 22:14); piercing like a trumpet (Revelation 1:10); roaring like the sound of rushing waters (Ezekiel 43:2); or as soft as a whisper (1 Kings 19:12).

All those visions and dreams from God that were experienced by people in the Bible were not meant just for those individuals who experienced them; they were meant for many people during that time and countless generations after them who would hear and read about those visions, dreams and revelations. God doesn't just speak to people in visions and dreams for the benefit of one person; God is always trying to communicate a message to many people or provide direction or help to many people through the visions and dreams of individuals.

When God gave pharaoh multiple dreams that terrified him, Joseph was brought before pharaoh to interpret his terrifying dreams. Joseph said to pharaoh, *"The reason the dream was given to Pharaoh in two forms is that the matter has been firmly decided by God, and God will do it soon."* (Genesis 41:32 NIV) Pharaoh's frightful dreams about 7 years of abundant crops followed by 7 years of drought and famine turned out to be not only for the benefit of pharaoh, but also for the benefit of Joseph, the Egyptians, the other surrounding nations affected by the famine, and ultimately, for the saving of all the children of Israel.

When the prophet Daniel was ushered into Nebuchadnezzar's court in Babylon to interpret the king's dream nightmare, Daniel told Nebuchadnezzar, *"No wise man, enchanter, magician or diviner can explain to the king the mystery he has asked about, but there is a God in heaven who reveals mysteries. He has shown King Nebuchadnezzar what will happen in days to come.* (Daniel 2:27–28 ESV) Daniel went on to say to Nebuchadnezzar, *"While your majesty was sleeping, you dreamed about the future; and God, who reveals mysteries, showed you what is going to happen."* (Daniel 2:29 GNT) Nebuchadnezzar's troubling dream of a statue made of four metals and clay was given to him not just for his benefit, but for the benefit of all generations who would hear this prophetic dream of future and End Time events.

Alexander the Great and the swift horse's hoofs of his conquering armies overpowered Asia like nightfall as the bloodshot eyes of enraged men now approached the holy city of Jerusalem to conquer and destroy it. However, God instructed the Jewish priests in a dream to open their city gates and leave the protection of Jerusalem's walled city dressed in their priestly garments and walk toward Alexander. Although this would mean certain death for the priests because several of the commanders and advisers of Alexander's armies were Samaritans, Phoenicians and Chaldeans who hated the Jews and wanted them destroyed and their city plundered, the anxious priests and the city citizens shuffled their fearful feet toward Alexander. To the shock and dismay of his commanders, Alexander dismounted his horse, calmly approached the priests and greeted them warmly, assuring them of his favor and peace. When the flustered commanders of Alexander's armies asked him why he changed his mind to annihilate the Jews, Josephus, the Jewish historian in his *Jewish Antiquities* 11.317–345, gives the reason for Alexander's changed behavior toward these priests and the Jews. Josephus tells us that Alexander told his commanders that he had a dream in Macedonia while on his campaign to conquer Asia. In his dream, Alexander saw a priest wearing the exact same garments that these Jewish priests were wearing. The priest in his dream told Alexander that God will give him victory over all of Asia, which God did, and over his upcoming battles with King Darius and all of Persia. Alexander saw the priest in his dream as a sign from God; and therefore, he graciously received these priests and all the Jews when he saw them wearing these exact same priestly robes. In other words, Alexander's dream from God was not just for Alexander's benefit; it was for the benefit of all his army and for all the Jews.

President Abraham Lincoln, a man of strong faith in God, also experienced multiple recurring dreams with strong premonitions throughout his presidency. Before almost every great event of the Civil War, such as the battles at Antietam, Gettysburg and Vicksburg, Lincoln told his cabinet members that he would dream the exact same dream of being on a *"singular and indescribable vessel that was moving with great rapidity toward a dark and indefinite shore"*. Lincoln also experienced this same dream just before his assassination. Three days before his death by a gunshot wound to the back of his head at the hands of his assassin, John Wilkes Booth, President Lincoln told his long-time friend and bodyguard, Ward Hill Lamon, that he dreamed he heard the sounds of people mourning in the White House. In his dream, he saw himself walking through the White House in search of the people who were mourning, and entered the door of the East Room. Lincoln said he was met with a frightening surprise of seeing a catafalque with a coffin containing a body lying in state, covered in funeral vestments, and throngs of people in the room gazing and mourning over the corpse whose face was covered. In his dream, Lincoln asked one of the soldiers guarding the corpse, *"Who was dead in the White House?"* to which the soldier replied, *"The President, he was killed by an assassin."* On the third day after this dream, President Lincoln died from his assassin's bullet. On April 18, 1865, Lincoln's body would lay in state in the East Room of the White House on a catafalque while the people filed into the East Room to view his body, mourning uncontrollably—just as Lincoln had dreamed about it three days earlier. But his death was not in vain nor were his dreams for all the people of our nation; especially his dream of a United States of America where slavery would be abolished.

Madam C. J. Walker (born Sarah Breedlove) was an African-American woman, philanthropist, political and social activist, and skincare and haircare products entrepreneur who, in the early 1900s, became the wealthiest African American woman in America; and is cited by the Guinness Book of Records as the first female self-made millionaire in the US. Suffering from skin disorders causing scalp ailments, severe dandruff and hair loss, she prayed to God asking for His help and a solution for her ailment and for other African American women who suffered from these same types of skin and hair problems. God answered her prayers by sending her an angel to give her a message in a dream. God used that dream to not only give her advice that would benefit her and make her a millionaire, God provided this message in her dream for the sake of many other people suffering from her same condition as well. In her own words, Walker said, "*He answered my prayer, for one night I had a dream, and in that dream a big, black man appeared to me and told me what to mix up in my hair. Some of the remedy was grown in Africa, but I sent for it, mixed it, put it on my scalp, and in a few weeks my hair was coming in faster than it had ever fallen out. I tried it on my friends; it helped them. I made up my mind to begin to sell it.*" Apparently, not all angels have white skin with flowing blond hair. Some of God's holy angels are black, just as Jesus Christ's skin color is not white but has a darker complexion, the same color as other Middle Eastern Jews; and his hair color was most likely black. In fact, when angels appear to you, they will oftentimes appear as the same race and complexion as you are, while speaking to you in your own language or dialect in both your dreams and in real life.

When God gave the Apostle John the prophetic vision of the Revelation of the Last Days while he was exiled on the Greek island of Patmos during the Christian persecution under the Roman emperor Domitian, our Lord Jesus told John in the vision, "*What you see, write in a book.*" (Revelation 1:11 NKJV) John himself said, "*Blessed is he who reads and those who hear the words of this prophecy* [the book of

Revelation], *and keep those things which are written in it; for the time is near.*" (Revelation 1:3 NKJV, bracketed emphasis mine) John's vision was not just for John; it was for all people for all time—it was for *you*.

Most of the greatest events in history recorded in the Bible were first foretold by God to someone in their dreams: the proclamation from God that the Jews would occupy the land of Israel and that all peoples on earth will be blessed through the Jews was given to Jacob in a dream (Genesis 28:11–15); the 400 years of Israelite bondage in Egypt and God's deliverance through Moses was foretold to Abraham in a dream (Genesis 15:13–14); the events that turned a slave prisoner into the governor over all of Egypt, being second only to pharaoh, that would save all Jews from famine and death was told to Joseph through his dreams (Genesis 37:2–9); the revelation that Mary's child was the Savior of the world was told to Joseph, Mary's husband, in his dream (Matthew 1:20–21); the history of our world's empires—from the glorious city of Babylon to the glorious kingdom of God on earth when Christ returns—was given to King Nebuchadnezzar in a dream (Daniel 2:1–46). Even the ultimate revelation that God did not consider Gentiles any less "unclean" as the Jews; that His divine plan was to save the Gentiles along with the Jews; and the power of the Holy Spirit falling upon the Gentiles for the first time was given to the Apostle Peter in the form of a dream that God repeated three times to Peter while he was sleeping. (Acts 10:10–48) And lest we forget something as important as the creation of woman (Eve), God did not perform this great creative miracle while man (Adam) was awake but while he was asleep. (Genesis 2:21–22)

Like so many people before me throughout recorded history who experienced dreams from God, I've written this book of what I saw in these recurring dreams for the purpose of others benefiting from this message God gave me in these dreams. This message from God through these dreams recorded in this book you are reading is not just for me; it was written for *you* as a message from God too.

Were these dreams that these other people in history and I experienced just a coincidence? Was it just bad pizza we ate that night before going to bed? I love pizza but that would mean I was eating bad pizza for seven nights in a row—I'm not that stupid. No, it wasn't a coincidence, bad pizza or something else we ate. It was the hand of God trying to reveal to us and you a message He wanted us to hear. These recurring dreams I dreamt and the life events that would follow after the pattern of these dreams was so important to God that He made sure I was well aware of it before I ever lived it out by repeating the exact same dream each night to me over a 1-week period. You could say it was prophetic because these dreams actually came true over and over again in my life just as I dreamt them over and over again each night. Jesus gave these same terrifying dreams to me seven nights in a row to make sure I got the message—but did I get the message? Will you get the message?

The strangest part about all of this is the fact that I wasn't even a Christian at the time when God gave me these dreams each night. It wasn't as if these dreams were some answer to my prayers because I didn't even know Jesus personally at the time; nor was I praying to God about anything. I never read the Bible before back then when I had these dreams, so I didn't even know what was in the Bible or that people in the Bible experienced visions and dreams from God. I wasn't asking God for help or a sign from heaven like some people might ask—I wasn't searching for God at the time. I was just another lost sinner living my life without God, the Bible, church or God's people when God repeated those same exact dreams to me each night. He chose to interrupt my life with these dreams without me ever asking or wanting Him or His dreams.

These dreams were so terrifying that I didn't want to surrender control to my pillow each night because these weren't just dreams; they were nightmares and I knew I would experience the same nightmare each night. And yet, there was nothing I could do about it. They just happened on their own—unannounced, uninvited and unwanted.

Imagine going to bed knowing you're going to have the same nightmare; knowing everything that's going to happen to you in that nightmare; you're scared to death each time in that nightmare; and you can't do anything about it. So you toss and turn each night with the fear and anxiety of knowing what awaits you behind the eyelids of your last conscious thought.

What is so strange to me about these dreams is I could see myself in the same setting acting out the same actions like unwanted reruns; I knew what was going to happen next with each nervous step because it was the exact same dream several nights in a row. Ever watched the same movie or cartoon repeatedly with a child because that was that child's favorite video? These dreams were like being forced to binge-watch your worst show repeatedly on Netflix; only the film was a horror movie that got worse and more terrifying towards the end each time you watched it.

But it all had to mean something, right? This couldn't possibly be happening to me for no reason at all! Like pharaoh or Nebuchadnezzar awakening from their dreams—their nightmares—shaking and trembling, asking themselves, "*What did all of this mean?*", I too came out of that nightmare each night trembling and wondering what is happening to me or what is about to happen to me.

My answer would not come in the form of a Joseph or a Daniel to interpret my dream for me. I didn't have the luxury of having every piece and puzzle of that terrifying experience explained to me the way Joseph interpreted pharaoh's dreams (Genesis 41:1–32) or Daniel revealing to King Nebuchadnezzar the meaning of his dreams (Daniel 2:26–45, 4:19–27). God appointed my own life to be my interpreter of my dreams. And only by living out that dream would I come to know and understand the fullness of its meaning as it related not only to me but to everyone else—including *you*. I had to live it out in my own life the way Joseph had to live out his dream of seeing his brother's sheaves bowing down to his sheaves (Genesis 37:5–8) and the sun (Joseph's father) and moon (Joseph's mother) and eleven stars (Joseph's brothers) bowing down to him (Genesis 37:5–9) before he could fully understand it's true revelation in his life. (Genesis 42:6, 14, 45:16–18)

I believe God took all this time, a large portion of my life really, to not only speak to me, but to speak through me—through my life—to other people like you. This is no coincidence that you are reading this book.

Christ told His disciple Peter that Satan asked to sift him and all the other disciples like wheat; and then Jesus ended this prophetic conversation he was having with Peter by saying, "*When you have turned back* [to Me], *strengthen your brothers.*" (Luke 22:31 NIV, bracketed emphasis mine) Like Peter who fell away and denied Christ three times before he could be useful in strengthening the brethren, I realize that what I had to go through would not be just for me; it would be for other people too—people like *you*—to strengthen you, to reveal something to you, to help you, and to edify and encourage you with this message of my dreams after I experienced in real life this prophetic dream conversation with the Lord. And God loved you so much that He used my life, the things He brought me through in life, to give you this all-important message you are about to read. Joseph's dream wasn't meant for Joseph alone; his dream was meant to impact his brothers and sisters and other people too. Pharaoh's and Nebuchadnezzar's dreams weren't meant only for them; it was meant for all the people. My dream was meant for you and other people to hear and understand too.

Just as the overall theme of the Book of Daniel is God's sovereignty over history, the overall theme of this book is the sovereignty of God weaved throughout the history of our lives. He's sovereign over the kingdoms of this world and He is sovereign over our lives. He wrote the book on the history of our lives—the Bible—and He knows every page of the book of your personal life. Like, Abraham, Joseph, Pharaoh and his two imprisoned butler and baker, Nebuchadnezzar, Alexander the Great, Abraham Lincoln, Madam C. J. Walker and the Apostle John; sometimes God wants you to know in advance what's ahead in your life. It just so happens He uses dreams to communicate that information to you.

Are you ready to hear the dream?

CHAPTER ONE

The Dream

I have a dream.
Dr. Martin Luther King Jr.

In the second year of his reign, Nebuchadnezzar had dreams; his mind was troubled and he could not sleep. So the king summoned the magicians, enchanters, sorcerers and astrologers to tell him what he had dreamed. When they came in and stood before the king, he said to them, "I have had a dream that troubles me and I want to know what it means."
Daniel 2:1–3 NIV

I Have a Dream

The thing I find most fascinating about Dr. Martin Luther King's famous *I Have A Dream* speech is not the man who gave the speech but the God behind the man who gave the speech. You see, Dr. King's 17-minute civil rights speech on the steps of the Lincoln Memorial during that 1963 *March on Washington for Jobs and Freedom* was originally written beforehand by his speechwriters Clarence B. Jones and Stanley Levinson; and the speech was thoroughly edited and debated over by Dr. King's team before echoing that speech into time immemorial on a warm August day while people cooled their bare feet in the reflecting pool.

The final speech that Dr. King planned to give to the crowd of 250,000 people at the Lincoln Memorial didn't even have his "*I Have A Dream*" portion in his written speech. But then the God behind the man who gave the speech showed up in the midst of his speech. After Dr. King stepped up to the stage to speak, the guest Gospel singer, Mahalia Jackson, who was already on the stage after singing to the crowd, shouted out to Dr. King saying, "*Tell them about the dream, Martin. Tell them about the dream.*" That's when it happened. In that moment, Dr.

King decided to extemporaneously add the now famous *I Have A Dream* portion of his speech while inspiring the crowd. This is what happens when God shows up in your dreams—God flips the normal, natural script of your dream into God's supernatural message to the people, just as God flipped Dr. King's prepared speech to give the people His message.

Joseph, a young man of seventeen, was tending the flocks with his brothers, the sons of Bilhah and the sons of Zilpah, his father's wives, and he brought their father a bad report about them. Now Israel loved Joseph more than any of his other sons, because he had been born to him in his old age; and he made an ornate robe for him. When his brothers saw that their father loved him more than any of them, they hated him and could not speak a kind word to him. Joseph had a dream, and when he told it to his brothers, they hated him all the more. He said to them, "Listen to this dream I had: We were binding sheaves of grain out in the field when suddenly my sheaf rose and stood upright, while your sheaves gathered around mine and bowed down to it." His brothers said to him, "Do you intend to reign over us? Will you actually rule us?" And they hated him all the more because of his dream and what he had said. Then he had another dream, and he told it to his brothers. "Listen," he said, "I had another dream, and this time the sun and moon and eleven stars were bowing down to me." When he told his father as well as his brothers, his father rebuked him and said, "What is this dream you had? Will your mother and I and your brothers actually come and bow down to the ground before you?" His brothers were jealous of him, but his father kept the matter in mind. (Genesis 37:2–11 NIV)

I was a 17-year-old in the 11th grade, my junior year of high school when the first of these dreams started happening to me in my sleep each night. I was still living with my parents in Wilmington, a small humble town in Southern California. These same dreams repeated themselves each night for 7 nights in a row. I've never dreamed these dreams or anything remotely similar to them ever again.

My dreams had some remarkable similarities to Joseph's dream retold in Genesis chapter 37. The Bible tells us that Joseph was also 17 years old when he first experienced his dream of his brother's bundles of grain bowing down to his bundle of grain. (Genesis 37:2, 5) Joseph's father, Israel (whose former name was Jacob), *loved Joseph more than any of his other sons, because he had been born to him in his old age.* (Genesis 37:3 NIV). My step-father who raised me since I was 5 years old was 68 years old when he married my mother—I too was raised and loved by my step-dad in his older age, who was now 80 years old when I started having these dreams at age 17. In my dreams I'm about to tell you, I saw myself outside in a field. In Joseph's dreams, he too was outside in a field. (Genesis 37:7)

Joseph's dreams of his brothers, mother and father bowing down to him (Genesis 37:10), however lofty they may have seemed at the time, appeared more like nightmares at first as their manifestations played out in the realities of his life. It was Joseph, not his brothers or parents, who appeared bowed in humility when he was made to fall down several times in a terrifying manner in his life: he was cast down into a pit by his own brothers as they plotted his death (Genesis 37:23); he was cast down by being sold into slavery by his brothers to a traveling caravan of Midianites who would drag him away from his home and family with no hope of ever seeing them again, a product of human trafficking (Genesis 37:28); and he was cast down by being thrown into a hopeless prison after being falsely accused by the wife of his slave master Potiphar while he was enslaved in Egypt. (Genesis 39:11–20)

In each of these dreams I dreamt, I was cast down each time in the most terrifying of ways. Like Joseph's brothers who grabbed hold of Joseph and cast him down into that pit while he pleaded helplessly for someone to rescue him; it was as if my dreams had arms that grabbed hold of me and threw me down mercilessly into a pit as I cried out in terror for someone to help me. As slavery and imprisonment seemed to haunt Joseph like a bad dream over and over again in his life, I was enslaved to the same dream-prison each night; and I would later find that I was imprisoned by these dreams manifesting repeatedly in my life.

Despite all of Joseph's trials, the Bible tells us that the Lord was with Joseph. (Genesis 39:2, 21) Every time Joseph was cast down, whether it was being thrown into a pit by his brothers, sold into slavery in a foreign land or cast into a prison with no hope of escape, the Lord was with Joseph to lift him up out of there each time. So it was in my dreams. Every time I was cast down into a terrifying pit in my dreams, the Lord was with me each time to deliver me out of that nightmare each night.

The First Recurring Dream

Each of these dreams is still just as clear in my mind today as the first night I dreamt them at age 17. As my last waking moment carried me off to that first night of sleep where dreams become shadows of reality, I found myself outside in a field at night running away from something. I didn't know what I was running away from or why, but my heart was racing with fear as I surveyed my surroundings. There were flashes of lightning tearing cracks in the darkened sky like warning signals of something ahead; and a strong, overpowering wind swept across the field that I could feel penetrating through my skin. The howling wind sounded like a pack of wolves marking their territory. An encroaching terror gripped me as my feet navigated through the tall blades of grass dancing wildly in that field. I looked back over my right shoulder, and through the darkness I could see a house off in the distance. I wondered what that house was as I ran in a direction away from it. At that moment, I fell over a cliff. I was in a terrifying free fall, twirling around fast as if I were a propeller of an airplane on takeoff. I tried fighting my fall thinking that would help as I cried out in terror but I was powerless as I fell. Then, just as quickly as I had fallen off that cliff, I awakened out of that nightmare; shaking and trembling the same way, no doubt, pharaoh or Nebuchadnezzar trembled after God released them from their dreams.

I'd never dreamt something as real and powerful as that in my life, but I was relieved to realize that it was only a nightmare, only a dream. I was glad and comforted myself in my waking reality knowing I didn't have to experience that nightmare again.

I could never have been more wrong.

Like Joseph, pharaoh of Egypt and King Nebuchadnezzar of Babylon, God had an important message about the future to give me; and He wasn't going to stop with just one dream to convey this message to me. The following night, the last thing I was thinking about was that nightmare of the previous night; but God had other plans. No sooner had I fallen asleep, I saw myself in the same field at night under the same conditions again—the wind was howling and blowing with hurricane force. What was so strange was that I immediately knew where I was in this dream—I knew I was in last night's nightmare! The same fear snaked around me with each crunch of grass under my feet. I glanced over my right shoulder and saw that exact same house again; still puzzled at what part that house had to play in this torment. And before I knew it, I had fallen over that same cliff again; a spinning horror show, terrified at tumbling to my death. Again I struggled to break free from the terror of that fall but something more powerful than my own willpower held me in its grasp. I felt like Jacob wrestling with the Lord at night during his journey back home (Genesis 32:24–25), only I was losing that wresting match. The more I fought to break out of this nightmare, the further downward I descended. I'd fallen further than I did in last night's nightmare; and then, as suddenly as this fall came, I was spit out of the mouth of my nightmare onto the shores of peaceful reality, like Jonah being spit out of that great fish after drowning in terror within its belly.

You can imagine my shock to find myself dreaming that same exact dream again. "*How is that possible?*" I thought. Perhaps it was just a coincidence that I dreamed the same dream two nights in a row, but I've never dreamed the same exact dream ever.

I was starting to feel a little uneasy about going to sleep the third night, barely convincing myself that it was only a dream. It couldn't possibly happen again—not three nights in a row! I closed my eyes hoping the Sandman brought an extra bucket of that magical dust to dump on my eyelids to give me pleasant dreams. No such luck. There I was again running in that same field of terror in the midst of that rushing windstorm; running from something I couldn't identify. All I saw through that darkness was that house when I looked over my right shoulder, and

5

down I went over that same cliff, spinning faster and further each time. The worst part of the dream was the tormenting spinning—I'm terrified of roller coaster rides, and this was one terrifying ride. The harder I fought to stop my fall, the further I twirled and dropped to what I thought was certain death. Again I had fallen further than my second dream before I awoke from this nightmare. I could tell I was dropping closer to the bottom of that death fall with each night's dream!

The Dark Bottom

I couldn't understand what was happening to me. Was I losing my mind? How could the same exact nightmare repeat itself over and over again each night? Why was I running in the dark through this field, and what was I running from? What was back there that had me running away through that field? And what's the deal with that house; why was that same house in each of these dreams? It's the only thing that seemed out of place in this nightmare because that house didn't appear threatening like everything else in this dream. Shouldn't I have been running to that house for protection instead of away from it to get out of that storm and away from that cliff?

I was now trying to analyze and figure out what this dream was all about and why. I lived in the city away from fields, mountains and cliffs, and I did not visit those types of locations nor desired to go there; so there was nothing during my daily thoughts and activities that might prompt such dreams of a field and cliffs. There was nothing in my life that looked remotely similar to those images I was seeing in my dream except maybe for that house because I lived in a house with my parents at the time. I wasn't experimenting with drugs or drinking alcohol that might influence these dreams. It seemed like fighting this nightmare only caused me to fall further each time. Should I let myself fall and see where it takes me? These types of thoughts were racing through my mind during the day while I began to fear and apprehensively wait the approaching night. It was like one of those old *Wolf Man* horror films where Lon Chaney tried to figure out during the day what he was going to do the next time a full moon appeared in the night's sky when he would transform into the nightmarish Wolf Man again. Each night was like that full moon to me when my dreams would transform into the same nightmare that would devour me again.

On the fourth night, I accepted my fate that I was going to dream the same nightmare again. In fact, I expected it to come that night like a prisoner who was led to his jail cell each night to receive more beatings by the guards. As weird as it sounds, the more I accepted my punishing captors, the less I resisted my tormenting dream cell. Once again, I drifted off to sleep only to find myself in the exact same dream again: the wind howling through the darkness of night in the field; the look over my shoulder at that house that seemed strangely out of place; and that terrifying, whirlwind fall off the cliff to my death. Once again, my normal reaction was to fight from falling but this only seemed to squeeze the jaws of death tighter around me as I spun to my death below.

But in the middle of my merciless descent, something told me to just let go, stop fighting and see what happens—all this in my sleep. So I stopped struggling and accepted my soon inevitable death at the quickly approaching dark bottom. Down I went further and further.

Then came the end—but it was not what I'd expected.

I could see the bottom now. There was total darkness all around except for this large perfectly round circle of light on the floor. It was a floor like a floor you might find in a house; it wasn't dirt, grassy or rocky ground that you would expect since I was outside in a field before falling over that cliff. There was no more howling wind, no more flashes of lightning, no more falling and spinning wildly out of control, and no more fear—just a silent calm.

Then I saw myself.

In the middle of that circle on the floor, I saw myself lying face up with my eyes closed, fully clothed and not moving. It was quite a shock to see myself lying there as if I was viewing myself from a distance of about 20 feet above myself like an out-of-body experience. From this strange vantage point, I just kept staring at my lifeless body to see if there was any movement but there was none. *"Was I dead?"* I pondered while examining myself like a doctor. I looked so much at peace and at rest.

So this is where my fall would take me, to this strange circle of light on the ground. I didn't see any injuries, mangled limbs from the fall or blood splattered anywhere. What does this mean? All these thoughts flashed through my mind in my sleep; and then suddenly, my roller coaster ride was over and I was awake again.

The following day, I felt more at ease knowing what was at the bottom of that terrifying fall—my still lifeless body resting motionless within a circle of light on the floor. I was hoping this revelation would mean the end of these repeating dreams; but once again, God was not done with these dreams or His message He wanted me to know and understand from these dreams. As I restlessly tossed in bed this fifth night in a row, I didn't feel the same level of apprehension of the impending "drop of doom" of that haunting dream because now I knew where I would end up if I just let myself go. I would end up resting motionless on the ground in the center of a mysterious circle of light.

As expected, the same nightmare visited my dreams again with its familiar dark, howling windy field. I was still running through the field from a fear unknown. The house was still there when I looked over my right shoulder and down I went over the cliff for the fifth time. At first, I struggled to fight my fall as usual, but then, while spinning downward wildly out of control, I remembered seeing myself at the bottom in that circle of light. I immediately stopped fighting the fall, and about three-fourths of the way down, I popped out of my dream.

A Lesson Learned from the Dream

I learned a valuable lesson that fifth night. I discovered a way to stop my fall without fighting my fall—I had to remember where this fall led me and simply let go and let the dream take its course. Armed with this new revelation, I decided I would try to use this information to break this cycle of my fall in these dreams. The following sixth night, the same dream reappeared again as if waiting for my arrival on the dream train. There I was running through the field at night as if I was running away from something. The pack of howling wind-wolves made their presence known blowing ferociously through me and that field. The glance backward over my shoulder revealed the same strange but now familiar house; and down I went over the cliff in another free fall death spin. Again, I started struggling to fight my fall but quickly remembered to let go and let the fall have its way with me. By the time I reached about halfway down, I popped out of that dream. Wow, it worked! For the first time, I'd fallen less than the previous night's dream. Not bad for someone in their sleep held captive by a recurring nightmare.

I didn't know how much more of this I could take but I was content to have made some slight progress in popping out of that fall in my dream sooner than the previous night's fall. I didn't know what was going on in my life. I was in survival mode; and the only thing I knew was that to survive falling in these recurring nightmares, I had to stop fighting and let go. It was the seventh night; one week of dreaming the same dream nightmare for 6 nights in a row. Once again, I drifted off to sleep, and for the seventh straight night I dreamed I was running through that darkened field, greeted by the howling wind, the house, the cliff and over I went twirling to my death. This time I didn't waste any time struggling. I didn't fight the fall and just let myself go. I immediately popped out of that dream before I fell one-fourth of the way down.

The next night it was over . . . completely over.

After I had mastered how to get myself out of that fall and pop out of those repeating nightmares, I never experienced those recurring dreams ever again in my life. That whole 7-night ordeal seem to come and go like some type of exercise or test that I had finally passed, as strange as that sounds. I couldn't tell you at the time what test I was taking or what exercise I had passed. I wasn't sure what I had learned except for that little slumber survival trick I learned in my dreams to just let go and let myself fall in order to break the cycle of my terrifying spinning falls which ended my dreams earlier each night. I also learned what was at the bottom of that fall—me lying there motionless on the floor in a circle of light; but I didn't know why I was there. Was there more to this than just a bunch of repeating dreams? Were these dreams some sort of message from God or premonition of things to come; a dream aberration or anomaly that extends beyond my normal expectations of sleep, like a strange aberration of my shadow that moves beyond what my own body had cast it to do?

Dreams from the Lord

Dr. Larry Dossey is an M.D. physician who graduated from the University of Texas Southwestern Medical Center in Dallas. He's also a decorated Vietnam veteran who served as a battalion surgeon during the Vietnam War, as well as having served as Chief of Staff of Medical City Dallas Hospital. He's a *New York Times* bestseller author of several books, including *Healing Words*: *The Power of Prayer and the Practice of Medicine*; *Prayer is Good Medicine*: *How to Reap the Healing Benefits of Prayer*; and *The Power of Premonitions*: *How Knowing the Future Can Shape Our Lives*; and has appeared several times on Oprah Winfrey's Network, radio show and magazine. Dr. Dossey states the 5 rules of thumb for taking premonitions from dreams seriously are when: (1) they warn you about a health crisis or death; (2) they seem so vivid and real to be a dream; (3) recurring dreams appear within the same night or succeeding nights; (4) the premonition comes with physical symptoms; and (5) the same premonition is experienced by another person close to you such as a spouse, loved one or close friend. I can tell you with certainty that those dreams I dreamt for 7 consecutive nights definitely fall into the first three categories of Dr. Dossey's 5 rules of thumb for taking premonitions seriously.

Although premonitions are strong feelings of anticipation of something good that's going to happen, they can also be an anxiety-filled forewarning of something bad that's about to happen. My dreams were anything but pleasant dreams of something good that was about to happen in my life. Everything in those dreams had the telltale signs of something foreboding, something evil, and something wrong that was going to take place in my future. As Brutus, the famous assassin of Julius Caesar said, *"Oh, that a man might know the end of this day's business ere it come!"* (Shakespeare's *Julius Caesar* play, Act 5, Scene 1) Both good and bad happenings make strange bedfellows in the world of dreams and premonitions.

Do you remember the Bible story told in Genesis chapter 40 of the pharaoh's chief cupbearer and chief baker who were thrown in prison because they had offended pharaoh of Egypt? Not only can it be lonely at the top, it can be dangerous at the top as well. They both had strange dreams that gave them a strong premonition, a deep sense of something foreboding that was about to happen in their future. They were troubled by their dreams because their dreams seemed too vivid and real, like a sign of something that was about to happen, but they didn't know what it was. They told their dreams to Joseph who also was held captive in the same prison with them.

This is how the cupbearer's dream went: *So the chief cupbearer told Joseph his dream. He said to him, "In my dream I saw a vine in front of me, and on the vine were three branches. As soon as it budded, it blossomed, and its clusters ripened into grapes. Pharaoh's cup was in my hand, and I took the grapes, squeezed them into Pharaoh's cup and put the cup in his hand."* (Genesis 40:9–10 NIV)

Then Joseph immediately interpreted the cupbearer's dream to him. *"This is what it means,"* Joseph said to him. *"The three branches are three days. Within three days Pharaoh will lift up your head and restore you to your position, and you will put Pharaoh's cup in his hand, just as you used to do when you were his cupbearer."* (Genesis 40:12–13 NIV) Joseph was telling the cupbearer that the dream he experienced was a premonition from God of something good that was about to happen in his life.

Delighted to hear Joseph's interpretation of the cupbearer's dream, the chief baker decided to tell Joseph his dream. *"I too had a dream: On my head were three baskets of bread. In the top basket were all kinds of baked goods for Pharaoh, but the birds were eating them out of the basket on my head."* (Genesis 4:16–17 NIV)

Then Joseph immediately interpreted the baker's dream to him. *"This is what it means," Joseph said. "The three baskets are three days. Within three days Pharaoh will lift off your head and impale your body on a pole. And the birds will eat away your flesh."* (Genesis 40:18–19 NIV) Apparently, the baker's box of Cracker Jacks didn't come with the toy he was expecting. Joseph was telling the baker that the dream he experienced was a premonition from God of something bad that was about to happen in his life. I doubt the baker got much sleep after that interpretation.

When the third day arrived, their premonitions were realized just the way Joseph had interpreted their dreams. The chief cupbearer's premonition in his dream was apparently good; and came true when he was restored to his former position in pharaoh's presence. The chief baker's premonition in his dream turned out to be bad just as Joseph told him; and came true when he was beheaded and impaled on a pole for birds to eat from his headless corpse. Who said the Bible was a boring book? It only took one dream for each of the chief cupbearer and chief baker for God to tell them about something that was about to happen in their future. But sometimes God gives multiple recurring dreams to confirm the message He wants to tell you in your dreams—good or bad.

When God wanted Pharaoh to know about the coming 7 years of a plentiful harvest followed by 7 years of drought and famine in Egypt and the surrounding nations, God gave Pharaoh multiple dreams filled with premonitions of something good that was about to happen followed by something foreboding and evil that was about to happen in his life. Genesis chapter 41 gives us the account: *Pharaoh had a dream: He was standing by the Nile, when out of the river there came up seven cows, sleek and fat, and they grazed among the reeds. After them, seven other cows, ugly and gaunt, came up out of the Nile and stood beside those on the riverbank. And the cows that were ugly and gaunt ate up the seven sleek, fat cows. Then Pharaoh woke up. He fell asleep again and had a second dream: Seven heads of grain, healthy and good, were growing on a single stalk. After them, seven other heads of grain sprouted—thin and scorched by the east wind. The thin heads of grain swallowed up the seven healthy, full heads. Then Pharaoh woke up; it had been a dream.* (Genesis 41:1–5 NIV)

Pharaoh's troubling dreams sent pharaoh's magicians and wise men scrambling for answers to pharaoh's dreams; but they could not interpret his dreams. When pharaoh heard from the chief cupbearer that Joseph, who was still in prison at the time, could interpret dreams, Joseph was brought before pharaoh to interpret his dreams. After interpreting pharaoh's dreams, Joseph told pharaoh why God gave him multiple dreams to communicate His message to him. Joseph told pharaoh, *"The reason the dream was given to Pharaoh in two forms is that the matter has been firmly decided by God, and God will do it soon."* (Genesis 41:32 NIV) As Dr. Dossey stated in the 5 rules of thumb for taking premonitions seriously, both pharaoh and I experienced multiple dreams that warned us about a health crisis or death; our dreams seemed so vivid and real to be a dream; and these recurring dreams appeared within the same night or succeeding nights.

Since pharaoh accepted Joseph's interpretation as a message from God, he was able to avert death and disaster that was headed their way in the form of 7 years of famine. What this tells us is that even though God may give you a dream about something that is a premonition of something to come; you can avert or change the outcome or effect of that dream even though those premonitions in your dreams come to pass in your life. In other words, the events God is telling you about in your dream can have an entirely different outcome than the way God shows it to you in your dream. Since pharaoh believed that there was danger approaching his nation, he did something about it to protect his people from that danger God warned him about in his dream. He listened to Joseph's advice on how to protect his kingdom from this 7-year famine that God was bringing upon the land. Pharaoh promoted Joseph and made him ruler over his entire kingdom, second only to pharaoh himself; and Joseph began the process of storing grain during the 7 years of plenty so that the Egyptians and the surrounding nations would have plenty of grain during the 7 years of famine. The actions that pharaoh and Joseph took in response to the dream averted death and destruction of the Egyptian kingdom; provided grain to other nations while making the Egyptians richer in the process; provided a means of preserving the lives of the Jews during this time of famine; and allowed Joseph's family of Jews to live in the good land of Goshen in Egypt during this difficult time. In the process, Joseph's dream also came to pass as Joseph's brothers bowed before Joseph as a ruler of Egypt. To ignore pharaoh's dream would have had devastating effects resulting in the death and disaster of the Egyptians, surrounding nations and the people of Israel.

Did you get that? I said in the introduction of this book that God does not give people messages through dreams just for the sake of the *one* but for the sake of *many*. But the messages God gives us is effective only when people listen to that message—only then can death and destruction be averted or avoided. If pharaoh had not taken to heart the message God was giving him in his multiple dreams, there would have been much death and destruction in Egypt and the surrounding nations because of the 7 years of famine.

This message I received from God in these multiple recurring dreams was a premonition of things to come that God had given me, but it wasn't just a message for me. It is a message for *you* and everyone else. Believe it, and you will be able to take the necessary actions in your life to avert and avoid the consequences of what is to come or is already happening in your life. Refuse to believe it and take the necessary steps to avert it, and you could suffer the consequences of what is to come.

When God gave King Nebuchadnezzar his terrifying dream of things to come through a statue made of four metals and clay, God's prophet Daniel was brought before the king to interpret his dream. Daniel revealed to Nebuchadnezzar that the statue's head of gold was his Babylonian kingdom (605 BC – 539 BC); the breast and arms of silver represented the Medes and Persians who would take over Babylon (539

BC – 331 BC); the belly and thighs of brass was Greece and Alexander the Great who conquered Babylon from the Medes-Persians (331 BC – 168 BC); the legs of iron represented Rome (168 BC – 476 AD) who conquered Babylon in 116 BC; the feet of iron and clay represented Satan's weakened kingdom of the End Times; and the rock—Christ—who will return to earth and strike the last End Times kingdoms of this world, destroying all previous kingdoms and establish the final everlasting kingdom of God on earth. (Daniel 2:31–45)

After Daniel explained to Nebuchadnezzar what God was going to do in the future based on the different metals and clay of the statue he saw in his dream, Daniel told Nebuchadnezzar, "*The great God has shown the king what will take place in the future. The dream is true and its interpretation is trustworthy.*" (Daniel 2:45 NIV) But that dream was not given to King Nebuchadnezzar just for his benefit; it was for the benefit of all generations who would hear this prophetic dream of future (most of which is now our past) and End Time events—it was for your benefit too.

And when God Himself decides to give you a message in the form of a dream or multiple dreams, you can be sure God is going to bring that message to pass in your life. God Himself said through the prophet Isaiah, "*Just as the rain and snow come down from heaven, and do not return there without watering the earth, making it bring forth and sprout, yielding seed for the sower and bread for eating, so will My message be that goes out of My mouth—it won't return to Me empty. Instead, it will accomplish what I desire, and achieve the purpose for which I sent it.*" (Isaiah 55:10–11 ISV) When God's word leaves His mouth and enters your dreams, His words will cause that dream to sprout and bear fruits of reality in your life.

So what can happen if someone doesn't listen to the message God is giving to a person in a dream? Well, let's take another look at King Nebuchadnezzar when God gave him another dream to warn him about his future and the future of his people. The eldest son of Chaldean King Nabopolassar who defeated the Assyrians with the help of the Medes, the great warrior-king Nebuchadnezzar II inherited the ancient Babylonian empire (located in modern-day Iraq 59 miles southwest of Baghdad) in 604 BC along with great wealth from his father Nabopolassar, and he used that bountiful wealth to make the Babylonian empire even greater.

Nebuchadnezzar went on to build the 2,200 acre city of Babylon, the largest city in the world at that time, that was subtly similar to the building campaign of the former people of Babylon who built the city and Tower of Babel, a ziggurat for the false god Marduk in the same Mesopotamian area (Genesis 11:1–9)—another foolish attempt by mankind and the devil to rival God's heavenly kingdom. In fact, the Babylonians in Nebuchadnezzar's day viewed their magnificent city of Babylon as paradise and the center of the world, similar to the thinking of the people who built the Tower of Babel in Babylon.

According to the ancient Greek historian Herodotus who was born in the Persian Empire in the 5th century BC, Nebuchadnezzar built Babylon's city boundaries as a square (13.794 miles on each side); just as God's heavenly city Jerusalem is shaped as a square cubicle (1379.4 miles in length, width and height) as recorded in Revelation 21:16—another vain attempt by mankind and the devil to mimic God's heavenly kingdom. Nebuchadnezzar built the 56-mile long brick walls surrounding Babylon, almost each brick with inscriptions that glorified his own name. These walls were so wide and massive that they had chariot races along the top; and Nebuchadnezzar had amassed so much gold that he had many of these walls overlaid with gold. This again was another subtle attempt by mankind and the devil to mimic the heavenly Jerusalem with its great high 72-yard thick walls of God's heavenly city Jerusalem that is made of precious stones with inscriptions of the names of the 12 apostles of Christ on the foundation stones of the wall. (Revelation 21:12, 17–20) Nebuchadnezzar also made impressive gates for his city including the glorious Ishtar gate, considered at one time as one of the Seven Wonders of the Ancient World that he dedicated to the false goddess Ishtar. Again, this was mankind's and Satan's poor attempt to rival the 12 pearly gates of the heavenly city Jerusalem that is guarded by angels, each gate made of a single solid pearl; and the heavenly city itself made of pure gold and its streets of pure gold. (Revelation 21:12, 21)

Nebuchadnezzar turned Babylon into a magnificent city of learning, culture, code of law which pre-dates the Mosaic Law, beautifully impressive structures, canals, waterways and opulent temples to his false god Marduk and other false gods. Nebuchadnezzar developed amazing feats of engineering that produced their multi-tiered Hanging Gardens watered by machinery that are considered one of the Seven Wonders of the Ancient World.

Nebuchadnezzar also defeated the Assyrians as well as the Egyptians, Palestinians and Syrians. He controlled trade routes and became the most powerful king with the most powerful kingdom during his 43-year reign. His kingdom had been highly exalted by Almighty God. However, Nebuchadnezzar's pride in his earthly kingdom and his own achievements became unacceptable before God when Nebuchadnezzar boasted of himself and his false god Marduk and other false gods as the reasons for his conquests, greatness and his magnificent city.

Because of his misplaced pride and worship of false gods, Almighty God decided to judge Nebuchadnezzar and strike him with a mental illness that would lead to his 7 years of insanity where he would be temporarily driven from his own kingdom as a madman; his hair grew out matted and long like eagle feathers; his nails grew out like birds claws; and he lived in the field, wet with dew and eating grass like an animal. (Daniel 4:28–34)

But before God would bring this disaster upon Nebuchadnezzar, the Lord God decided to send His holy one, also known as messenger or watcher which is an angel, from heaven to give Nebuchadnezzar a message in the form of a dream of his impending doom in the future.

Question for you: Why did God give Nebuchadnezzar a dream about what was going to happen in his future? Why didn't God just do it without any warning from a dream nightmare since it was apparent God already knew Nebuchadnezzar was sinful and prideful and needed to be humbled?

The answer is God does not desire to punish people, nor does He desire the death of sinners—He'd rather people repented of their sins and not be punished or put to death, including death in hell. God says in Ezekiel 18:32 NLT, "*Do you think that I like to see wicked people die?*" *says the Sovereign LORD. "Of course not! I want them to turn from their wicked ways and live.*" The Apostle Peter tells us, "*The Lord is not slow about His promise, as some count slowness, but is patient toward you, not wishing for any to perish but for all to come to repentance.*" (2 Peter 3:9 NASB) God prefers to warn people of future calamity in order to give them the opportunity to take the necessary actions—repenting of sins as Nebuchadnezzar needed to do or take some other necessary action such as storing up grain as Joseph did—in order to avert the death, danger or disaster headed their way. One of the reasons God gives dreams to people is so that they have the opportunity to change or avert the negative outcomes shown them in the dream that will become a reality in their lives in the future.

Nebuchadnezzar speaks of the dream nightmare God gave him this way: "*I had a dream that made me afraid. As I was lying in bed, the images and visions that passed through my mind terrified me.*" (Daniel 4:5 NIV) I know that feeling oh so well from the recurring dreams God gave me of falling off that cliff. In the dream God gave Nebuchadnezzar, he saw himself in the form of a magnificent, beautiful tall tree in the center of a field (Babylon, the center of the world at the time). Once again, God used a field backdrop of Nebuchadnezzar's dream just He did with Joseph's and my dream. Then Nebuchadnezzar saw a messenger (an angel) coming down from heaven to make this proclamation: "*Cut down the tree* [Nebuchadnezzar] *and trim off its branches; strip off its leaves and scatter its fruit. Let the animals flee from under it and the birds from its branches. But let the stump and its roots, bound with iron and bronze, remain in the ground, in the grass of the field. Let him be drenched in the dew of heaven, and let him live with the animals among the plants of the earth. Let his mind be changed from that of a man and let him be given the mind of an animal, till seven times* [7 years] *pass by for him.*" (Daniel 4:14–16 NIV, bracketed emphasis mine) Talk about a premonition of something bad that is about to happen in your future! I think I prefer my nightmare field experience in my multiple dreams from the Lord instead of Nebuchadnezzar's nightmare field experience in his single dream from God.

Again, the point to take away from this is that God does not give dreams for the benefit of only the person who received the dream from God but for many people to hear and learn from the message in the dream. And if neither the person who had the dream nor those who hear about the dream do anything to change or avert the outcome of the dream, it will manifest itself in real life unhindered. This is why the angel who made the proclamation in Nebuchadnezzar's dream also gave a reason for his dream and the judgment by God upon Nebuchadnezzar: "*The decision is announced by messengers* [angels], *the holy ones* [angels] *declare the verdict* [from God], *so that the living* [people on earth] *may know that the Most High* [God] *is sovereign over all kingdoms on earth and gives them to anyone He wishes and sets over them the lowliest* [humblest] *of people.*" (Daniel 4:17 NIV, bracketed emphasis mine) In other words, the message in Nebuchadnezzar's dream from God was not just for Nebuchadnezzar but for every person on earth—it was a message for *you and me.* The angel's message to Nebuchadnezzar is clear: God controls all things; and God blesses those who are humble, and humbles those who are proud. God tells us in His word, "*Before destruction a man's heart is haughty, but humility comes before honor*" (Proverbs 18:12 ESV) and "*I hate pride and arrogance, evil behavior and perverse speech.*" (Proverbs 8:13 NIV) Solomon, the wisest man in the world said, "*Pride leads to disgrace, but with humility comes wisdom*" (Proverbs 11:2 NLT) and "*Pride goes before destruction, and a haughty spirit before a fall.*" (Proverbs 16:18 NKJV)

Going back to my original question: *What can happen if someone doesn't listen to the message God is giving to a person in a dream?* The answer is the dream's message will play itself out in the reality of that person's life and in the lives of other people. This is what happened to King Nebuchadnezzar and the people of his kingdom because he did not listen to the warning from God in his dream, nor did he listen to Daniels advice to avert and change the calamity that was pronounced upon him by God in that dream. Daniel advised the king, "*So then, your majesty, follow my advice. Stop sinning, do what is right, and be merciful to the poor. Then you will continue to be prosperous.*" (Daniel 4:27 GNT) Instead, King Nebuchadnezzar chose to not listen to the dream from God and suffered the consequences of that dream becoming a reality in his life. Nebuchadnezzar experienced 7 years of insanity and lost it all during those 7 years just as God prophesied it in his dream. (Daniel 4:28–37)

As with the prophet Daniel, it is my prayer that you too will accept the advice I'm about to give you as I share with you the interpretation and God's message to you from my recurring dreams I received from the Lord.

CHAPTER TWO

The Interpretation of the Dream

Deep into that darkness peering, long I stood there, wondering, fearing, doubting, dreaming dreams no mortal ever dared to dream before.

Edgar Allan Poe

It is God who gives the ability to interpret dreams . . . Tell me your dreams.

Genesis 40:8 GNT

Prophecy, Visions and Dreams in the End Times

Among the many people throughout history who experienced dreams from God, Edgar Allan Poe was one of them who not only paid attention to his dreams; he wrote some of them down as poems, such as *Dream-Land* and *A Dream Within A Dream*. Many of his dreams were actually nightmares like mine that inspired him to write many of his poems and short stories. In his 1839 essay on *An Opinion On Dreams*, Edgar Allan Poe soberly wrote, *"That dreams, or, as they were then generally called, visions, were a means of supernatural instruction, if we believe the bible at all, is proved by Jacob's dream, the several visions of Ezekiel and other prophets, as also of later date, the Revelations to Saint John; and there appears no reason why this mode of divine communication should be discontinued in the present day."*

According to God's word, prophesying the word of God, dreaming dreams from God and seeing visions from God are part of the signs we are in the Last Days—which many believe is the *present day* in which we live that Edgar Allan Poe is referring to. The Last Days is also referred to as Day of the Lord, Final Days, End of Days, Latter Days, End Times, End of Times, Last Time, end of the world, and end of the ages. All of these names fall under the subject of Eschatology which is the part of theology that studies end-of-world and end-of-mankind scenarios, death, judgment after death, the finality of souls, and the ultimate manifestation of God's kingdom reign on earth. Prophecy, dreams and visions from God are part of the modus operandi of Last Days events—it's supposed to happen in the End Times.

"And in the last days it shall be, God declares, that I will pour out my Spirit on all flesh, and your sons and your daughters shall prophesy, and your young men shall see visions, and your old men shall dream dreams." (Acts 2:17 ESV)

"And it shall come to pass afterward, that I will pour out my Spirit on all flesh; your sons and your daughters shall prophesy, your old men shall dream dreams, and your young men shall see visions. Even on the male and female servants in those days I will pour out my Spirit. And I will show wonders in the heavens and on the earth, blood and fire and columns of smoke. The sun shall be turned to darkness, and the moon to blood, before the great and awesome day of the LORD comes." (Joel 2:28–31 ESV)

It doesn't matter if you don't believe in prophecy, dreams or visions. What matters is God said these things would be among the signs we will see in the Last Days. Why do we need prophecy, dreams and visions in the End Times? Because in the End Times, people need direction; and that's what prophecy, dreams and visions are for—they are directions, signposts pointing us to Christ in the Last Days. The Bible tells us *"the testimony of Jesus is the spirit of prophecy."* (Revelation 19:7 NKJV)

In the Last Days, Satan will do everything he can to deceive and misdirect people away from God the way he deceived Adam and Eve in the Garden of Eden. In the book of Revelation, God pulls back the curtain to the spiritual realm to let us see what is taking place in the battle between good and evil and Satan's desire to deceive mankind in the Last Days. Revelation tells us *"Then war broke out in heaven. Michael* [the archangel] *and his angels* [one-third holy angels he is in charge of] *fought against the dragon* [Satan], *and the dragon* [Satan] *and his angels* [the one-third fallen angels that rebelled along with Satan against God] *fought back. But he* [Satan] *was not strong enough, and they* [Satan and his fallen angels] *lost their place in heaven. The great dragon was hurled down—that ancient serpent called the devil, or Satan, who leads the whole world astray. He was hurled to the earth, and his angels with him . . . But woe to the* [people on] *earth and the sea, because the devil has gone down to you! He is filled with fury, because he knows that his time is short."* (Revelation 12:7–9, 12 NIV, bracketed emphasis mine) Satan is the one who leads the whole world astray in these Last Days because he knows his time is short before Christ returns to the earth and casts him and all his fallen angels into the lake of fire to be tormented throughout all eternity along with all unbelievers that he deceived into not believing in Christ as their Savior and Lord. So naturally, you want to be on your guard in these Last Days and not believe every Prophet Tom, Reverend Dick or Pastor Harry that comes along and tells you they received a dream, vision, message or prophecy from God. Satan has a counterfeit for everything that God is doing, including counterfeiting Christ with his own antichrists to deceive the nations into believing his antichrists are the real Christ in these Last Days. The Apostle John warns us, *"Dear friends, do not believe everyone who claims to speak by the* [Holy] *Spirit. You must test them to see if the spirit they have comes from God. For there are many false prophets in the world."* (1 John 4:1 NLT, bracketed emphasis mine)

God didn't mince words when it came to prophets and dreamers of dreams who were being used by Satan to deceive people to draw them away from the Lord. When God was giving His laws to the Jews after He brought them out of slavery in Egypt, God commanded through Moses, *"If a prophet, or one who foretells by dreams, appears among you and announces to you a sign or wonder, and if the sign or wonder spoken of takes place, and the prophet says, 'Let us follow other gods' (gods you have not known) 'and let us worship them', you must not listen to the words of that prophet or dreamer. The LORD your God is testing you to find out whether you love Him with all your heart and with all your soul. It is the LORD your God you must follow, and Him you must* revere. *Keep His commands and obey Him; serve Him and hold fast to Him. That prophet or dreamer must be put to death for inciting rebellion against the LORD your God, who brought you out of Egypt and redeemed you from the land of slavery. That prophet or dreamer tried to turn you from the way the LORD your God commanded you to follow. You must purge the evil from among you.*" (Deuteronomy 13:1–5 NIV)

Our loving heavenly Father is making sure we are headed in the right direction during these Last Days so that we aren't led astray and lost on Satan's path of unbelief in Christ. *There is a way that seems right to a man, but its end is the way of death.* (Proverbs 16:25 NKJV) So it shouldn't be surprising when people are prophesying, dreaming dreams or seeing visions from God today because we're in the Last Days. Nor should it surprise you that Satan's is trying to copy what God is doing because Satan always wants to copy God in order to *be like God.* It's par for the course. So when I share with you the fact that I've had recurring dreams from God, it really doesn't matter if you believe me or not. I'm just one of many signposts that God is giving us to make us aware that we are living in the End Times while pointing us to Christ who is the right Way to take to heaven. God said, "*Hear now My words: If there is a prophet among you, I the LORD, shall make Myself known to him in a vision. I shall speak with him in a dream.*" (Numbers 12:6 NASB)

One of the telltale signs or indicators that you've experienced a message from God in the form of a dream is that the dream will repeat itself. God will repeat the dream to you to get your attention, to wake you up in your dream as if to say, "*Hey, I'm talking to you, pay attention!*" That's why Joseph and pharaoh experienced multiple dreams. That's why I experienced multiple dreams instead of just one dream.

When God gives you a dream to reveal things to come in the future, it's like looking at yourself or your life in a warped mirror and seeing a different reflection of yourself or your life in the future; not a reflection of yourself or your life in the present. That's what it was like for Joseph when God showed him his future in the mirror of his dreams that reflected his family members in the form of sheaves bowing down to him.

That's what pharaoh of Egypt saw in his dream mirror when God showed him his future in the shape of cows and heads of grain. That's what God was doing when He showed King Nebuchadnezzar his terrifying future reflection of a tree stump—he would be overtaken with insanity; and a statue when his Babylonian kingdom would be overtaken by the Medes and Persians in 539 BC. God was also showing me a reflection of my future of falling in His dream mirrors. *"For now we see only a reflection as in a mirror; then we shall see face to face. Now I know in part; then I shall know fully, even as I am fully known."* (1 Corinthians 13:12 NIV)

God Expects You to Interpret and Understand His Dreams

When God gives you a message in the form of dreams, He expects you to understand the message or premonition He is trying to convey to you in that dream. God doesn't just give you a message in a dream and then says to you, *"Go figure it out on your own"* like you're on some *Jeopardy* or *Wheel of Fortune* game show. No, you can be sure if God gave you the dream, God is going to reveal to you what that dream means. God will help you understand His message in your dream through His Holy Spirit speaking to your heart and mind, through His written word in the Bible, and through other people and circumstances. After all, God has a lot riding on you understanding that message in your dream because it is most likely a message meant not only for your benefit but for the benefit of other people—just as with Joseph, pharaoh and Nebuchadnezzar.

When God revealed to Daniel the mystery and interpretation of King Nebuchadnezzar's dream, the Bible tells us *then Daniel praised the God of heaven and said: "Praise be to the name of God for ever and ever; wisdom and power are His. He changes times and seasons; He deposes kings and raises up others. He gives wisdom to the wise and knowledge to the discerning. He reveals deep and hidden things; He knows what lies in darkness, and light dwells with Him. I thank and praise You, God of my ancestors: You have given me wisdom and power, You have made known to me what we asked of You, You have made known to us the dream of the king."* (Daniel 2:19–23 NIV)

25

God is constantly trying to communicate with us, especially in these Last Days; but oftentimes, in our busy lives we don't sit still long enough to recognize when He is present and trying to speak to us. Therefore, He uses dreams to get our attention and speak to us. That quiet solitary place where our work and play, worries and regrets, kids and pets, TV shows and fake news, iPhones and social media cannot follow us. That isolated getaway on the highest mountain of dreams, in the deepest forest of sleep where God alone can have our full undivided attention with no one and nothing around to interfere with what He has to say to us. The Bible tells us, *"God speaks again and again, though people do not recognize it. He speaks in dreams, in visions of the night, when deep sleep falls on people as they lie in their beds. He whispers in their ears and terrifies them with warnings. He makes them turn from doing wrong; He keeps them from pride. He protects them from the grave, from crossing over the river of death."* (Job 33:14–18 NLT)

One person who had a lot on his mind was Jacob who was on the run from his brother Esau who wanted to kill him after Jacob cheated Esau out of his birthright. (Genesis 27:41–43) When God revealed Himself to Jacob's crowded thoughts in a dream while he was en route to his uncle Laban's territory for safety, Jacob awoke from that dream from the Lord and said, *"Surely the LORD is in this place, and I wasn't even aware of it!"* (Genesis 28:16 NLT) It's only after God has revealed Himself to us in our dreams and spoken to us in our sleep that we realize He was there in our lives all this time trying to communicate with us.

Joseph, the betrothed husband of Mary who was pregnant with Jesus by the Holy Spirit, must have had a mind full of doubts and worries as he contemplated divorcing Mary quietly for this—in his mind—unwanted pregnancy. The troubling thoughts and voices racing through his mind were too loud for God to communicate His presence and plan He had for Joseph, Mary and the entire world; therefore, God waited until Joseph was sound asleep. That's when God dispatched a messenger (an angel) with a heavenly telegram to the calm, quiet residence of Joseph's dreams saying, *"Joseph son of David, do not be afraid to take Mary home as your wife, because what is conceived in her is from the*

Holy Spirit. She will give birth to a son, and you are to give him the name Jesus, because He will save His people from their sins." (Matthew 1:20–21 NIV) Once Joseph was sound asleep, God was able to give Joseph the direction he needed through a dream. That message of a Savior would not only benefit Joseph but all mankind.

Dreams from God are for One and Many

They say that hindsight is 50-50. That is certainly the case when it comes to the interpretation of my multiple recurring dreams from the Lord Jesus at age 17. Some 40 plus years later after experiencing those dreams, I can tell you for a fact that those dreams became a reality in my life. I actually experienced those falls over that cliff in more ways than one, only not in the literal way that it appeared to me in those dreams. But isn't that how God operates in dreams? When Joseph's dream materialized in real life, it wasn't the stalks of grain of Joseph's brothers that bowed down to Joseph's stalks of grain; it was Joseph's brothers themselves in the flesh that bowed down to Joseph. When the chief baker's dream became real life three days later, it wasn't three baskets of bread and other baked goods that birds were eating from the top of the baker's head; it was the top of the baker's headless corpse that the birds were eating from. So it was with my dreams.

Just as God would always ensure the dreams He gives not only benefit the person to whom He gave the dream but also other people; God oftentimes has different messages in the interpretation of the dream: one message is for the dreamer of the dreams and the other message for people who would hear about the dream. Let me explain.

When Joseph experienced his multiple dreams of his brothers stalks of grain bowing down to Joseph's stalks of grain, there were two messages given in the interpretation of that dream. One message in the interpretation of the dream was for Joseph, the dreamer of the dream. This first message in the dream interpretation meant Joseph would be exalted above his brothers. The other message in the interpretation of the dream was for Joseph's brothers who heard the dream. This second message in the dream interpretation meant Joseph's brothers would humbly bow before Joseph at some future time.

In the same way, God has given two different messages in the interpretation of these multiple recurring dreams I experienced. The first message in the dream interpretation would tell me about things that would happen to me in my future. The second message in the dream interpretation is for everyone else—including *you*—who is hearing about these dreams. This second message is what God wants you to know about your future.

The Dream Fulfilled: God's Message to Me

After I experienced those recurring dreams of falling off that cliff for 7 nights in a row, I never dreamed those nightmares ever again. I thought that episode in my life was over and I could move on with my life as a normal 17-year-old in his junior year of high school; but something strange and totally unexpected happened to me the following year. In my senior year of high school, I started to develop major depression out of nowhere.

Perhaps it was attributed to a head concussion I suffered while playing football at junior high school when I was 15 years old, and had to undergo brain surgery to release pressure from the swelling on my brain. Whatever the reason, I was experiencing all the signs of clinical depression: a persistent feeling of sadness, helplessness and hopelessness; an overall feeling of melancholy and loss of interest or pleasure in all activities; poor appetite and lack of concentration; repeatedly going over negative thoughts with the inability to see positive solutions; social isolation and suicidal thoughts.

Major depression is a well understood malady in the medical community. According to the Mayo Clinic, these symptoms of severe depression are very common, affecting more than 3 million people in the US each year. The *Journal of the American Medical Association* states the incidences of depression among females in the US is 26% compared to 8–12% for males—and no one is immune to it. For those of you who have or have experienced this level of depression, take heart. You're not alone as you can see from these statistics; and there is proven treatment for your depression—you don't have to go it alone. You can receive treatment from the medical community or you can receive treatment the way I did as I'll explain to you in the interpretation of my dream.

This severe depression I was experiencing at age 18 caused me to fall out of society, and I lost all interest in family or friends. I was skipping classes in school because I'd lost all interest in the subjects, the people and activities in school. I didn't want to see anyone and I didn't want anyone to see me; therefore, I stayed inside my parent's home most of the time. It was as if my life was falling over a cliff over and over again with each passing day as I fell further and further into a pit of depression with my hopes, my peace and my joy spinning wildly out of control—just like in that dream nightmare I experienced over and over again the previous year. In my troubling thoughts, I tried toughing it out by fighting off the depression; but the harder I tried fighting the depression, the deeper I sunk into depression—just like in my dreams. My family members tried to console and encourage me but it didn't do any good. I had fallen too far down that dark bottomless pit of depression for them to reach me. Week after week, month after month it pulled me down further—I couldn't shake myself free of this depression. For those of you who have experienced severe depression, you'll understand what I'm about to say: depression is like the canvas of your world of color suddenly turned black and white—a gray joyless world of no peace or laughter. I went through the first half of my senior year of high school this way, skipping more classes until I finally dropped out of high school midway through my senior year. Neither I nor my family knew what was happening to me; nor could I explain why—just like in my dreams.

Since I didn't know what to do, I decided to do the same thing I did in my recurring dreams; and that was to just stop fighting the depression and let myself go and see where it would take me. The result would be just as amazing as when I let myself go in my dream nightmares.

Several months had passed and my depression didn't seem to be getting any better. One day, while my thoughts of depression plagued me in my parent's home, I decided to go over to a bookshelf and read a book. I had no interest in any activities, including reading books, but for some reason, this particular day I felt the need to read a book. As my eyes swept across the books on the shelves, I noticed a Bible. Although my family and I were raised in the Catholic faith, I had never read the Bible before. I had stopped attending church several years ago and really had no interest in God even before I was experiencing this depression. As I thumbed through the pages too quickly to make out the words, I thought to myself, "*Why not take a look at what this book is about?*"

Just like any other book I'd read in the past, I flipped the pages to the beginning and began reading at Genesis. The moment I started reading, my interest was immediately piqued at what this book had to say. Perhaps it was because I'd never read the Bible before; the stories in that book amazed me. It was different from any other book I'd read. I wondered, "*Did these things really happen? Can this God in this book be for real?*" Like a curious cat in a paper bag, I jumped into this book each day reading one chapter at a time, one book of the Bible after another.

That's when I noticed something happening to me.

I didn't realize it at first but gradually I started noticing that I wasn't feeling as depressed as I usually felt. I couldn't put my finger on it; I could just tell something was changing for the better on the inside of me the more I read that Bible. My mind and thoughts started getting clearer and calmer each day. My disposition started getting brighter. The only thing I could attribute to me feeling better was that book—the Bible—that I was reading; so I decided to keep on reading it each day.

Then one day while flipping through TV channels, I stumbled upon a Christian TV station. I'd never watched Christian television before, but I noticed they were talking about some of the similar things I read in that Bible; so I decided to start listening to what they had to say. Again, I noticed the more I listened to the words of the Bible spoken by those people on TV, the better I felt inside myself; so I kept watching them each day too.

They kept talking about this Jesus who died for my sins and rose again for me; and if I confessed my sins and asked Jesus into my heart, all my sins would be forgiven and I'd get to go to heaven. They would ask people watching their program to pray with them to receive Christ into their hearts; but all this Jesus stuff was new to me—I wasn't ready to pray about anything. The only Jesus I knew was the baby Jesus in the manger; not this Jesus who died on the cross for my sins, rose from the dead and was alive today asking me to receive Him into my heart and have a relationship with Him. But I decided to keep watching them because it somehow made me feel better.

Then came the day when I decided to pray that prayer with those folks on TV to accept Jesus into my heart. One day, when those people on TV began saying a prayer to receive Christ into their hearts, I got on my knees in front of that television and prayed with them to receive Christ into my heart.

That's when the miracle happened!

The moment I finished praying that prayer, I immediately felt all of my depression completely fall off of me like a dead leaf falling off a branch. It wasn't like my depression took days or weeks to disappear; I mean it instantly disappeared! I popped out of that depression just as quickly as I popped out of my recurring nightmares. It was like a 500 pound gorilla just got lifted off of my mind the second I finished praying that prayer to receive Christ into my heart. My thoughts immediately became clear and my heart, mind and soul was immediately filled with more joy and peace than I had ever experienced in my entire life. I was completely free of depression from that moment on; and I have never been depressed ever again. *Jesus said, "You will know the truth, and the truth will set you free."* (John 8:32 HCSB)

I started smiling and laughing again! I could see colors again! Everything was bright and beautiful again! I started thinking positive thoughts again; all the negative thoughts that plagued me just moments ago had completely disappeared from my mind. My mind was fully restored to me—no; my mind felt better than it had ever felt in my life! I was like King Nebuchadnezzar after he came out of his 7-year insanity that God warned him about in his dreams. My 7 nights of falling had finally ended just as Nebuchadnezzar's 7 years of insanity finally ended. When Nebuchadnezzar snapped out of his insanity, he said *"At the end of that time, I, Nebuchadnezzar, raised my eyes toward heaven, and my sanity was restored. Then I praised the Most High; I honored and glorified Him who lives forever. His dominion is an eternal dominion; His kingdom endures from generation to generation. All the peoples of the earth are regarded as nothing. He does as He pleases with the powers of the heaven and the peoples of the earth. No one can hold back His hand or say to Him, "What have You done?" At the same time that my sanity was restored, my honor and splendor were returned to me for the glory of my kingdom. My advisers and nobles sought me out, and I was restored to my throne and became even greater than before. Now I, Nebuchadnezzar, praise and exalt and glorify the King of heaven, because everything He does is right and all His ways are just. And those who walk in pride He is able to humble."* (Daniel 4:34–37 NIV)

I went from the saddest person in my family to the happiest person in my family instantly; and it was all because Jesus was now in my heart and life. He completely healed my mind, my heart and my soul. It was an amazing, immediate transformation. Now I too, like Nebuchadnezzar, praise and exalt and glorify Jesus, the King of kings and Lord of lords. I was completely at peace and rest—just like that image I saw of myself lying in that round circle of light at the bottom of that great frightening fall off that cliff in my dreams. However, my fall over this cliff into this dark pit of depression led to rest for my soul in my salvation in Christ. The prophet Isaiah said of God, *"You keep him in perfect peace whose mind is stayed on You, because he trusts in You."* (Isaiah 26:3 ESV)

I'd reached the bottom in life through this depression just like I'd reached the bottom in those recurring dreams from God just a year prior. And the lesson I learned from this fall to the bottom of life is that Jesus Christ is at the bottom to catch you and break your fall. If things in life are leaving you feeling helpless and hopeless, give it to Jesus who said, *"Come to Me, all you who are weary and burdened, and I will give you rest. Take My yoke upon you and learn from Me, for I am gentle and humble in heart, and you will find rest for your souls. For My yoke is easy and My burden is light."* (Matthew 11:28–30 NIV) When you find yourself falling in life, stop fighting it yourself and call out to Jesus and let yourself go in His hands—He will catch you. He's been waiting all this time at the bottom for you to seek him, to call out to Him, and to receive Him into your heart. If you don't, you'll just keep falling. Don't struggle with what is trying to take you down in life; let go and let Jesus deliver you from your nightmare in life. Let go and let God handle it.

My family couldn't believe the 180 degree change in me. I was a new person in Christ and everyone in my family could see that I was a new person. I didn't know it at the time but I would learn later that the Bible says, *"Anyone who belongs to Christ has become a new person. The old life is gone; a new life has begun."* (2 Corinthians 5:17 NLT) My family members wanted to know how this miraculous change occurred in me. Naturally, I wanted them to know about this Christ I found at the bottom of my fall. After all, this Good News wasn't a message just for me; it was for them as well—just as the message in the dreams God gives us is not just for us to benefit from but for other people to benefit from as well. So I started sharing Christ with my family members and they too gave their hearts to Christ.

Not only did God change me on the inside; He changed me on the outside as well. Since I missed my high school graduation, I attended night school for one month and completed my requirements to receive my high school diploma. I went on to serve 20 years in the US Air Force while earning a Bachelor of Science degree; and I did it all with a smile on my face and joy in my heart because of Christ in my life.

Of course, for me to tell you how I benefited from the message in this dream is only half the message of this true story of dreams from God. The second, and perhaps more important, reason why God chose me to experience these same recurring dreams 7 nights in a row was because he wanted me to pass on to you His message I'm about to share with you in this book. The other half of this true story is how this message from these dreams from God benefits you. This message will shake you to your core, awaken you in your spirit, warn you about what will happen in your future, and give you the direction God wants you to hear from Him—just as my message from this dream did for me.

Are you ready to hear your message from God? The remainder of this book is devoted to God's message to you through my recurring dreams.

The Dream Fulfilled: God's Message to You

In the 15th chapter of the book of Luke in the Bible, Jesus teaches us through the parable of the prodigal son—the life lessons of a prodigal son. Jesus told the crowds, "*A certain man had two sons. And the younger of them said to his father, 'Father, give me the portion of goods that falls to me.' So he divided to them his livelihood. And not many days after, the younger son gathered all together, journeyed to a far country, and there wasted his possessions with prodigal living*". (Luke 15:11–13 NKJV)

To give you a better understanding of a prodigal life, other versions of the Bible describe this son's prodigal living by saying he:

"*squandered his wealth in wild living*" (NIV)
"*wasted his estate, living prodigally*" (BSB)
"*squandered his property in reckless living*" (ESV)
"*squandered his estate in foolish living*" (CSB)
"*wasted everything he had on a wild lifestyle*" (GWT)
"*squandered his estate with loose living*" (NASB)
"*wasted all his money in wild living*" (NLT)

34

I'd like to tell you that I faithfully served and followed God all the days of my Christian life since the day Jesus healed me of my deep depression and saved my soul. That's simply not the way my life played out as a Christian. I was more like this prodigal son in the parable that Jesus gave. Over the years, I had backslid and fallen away from God and church more times than I care to remember. Falling away from God and church would be a constantly recurring theme throughout my Christian life—just like in my recurring dreams where I kept falling over that cliff.

This recurring theme of falling over a cliff in the dreams God gave me carries with it a heavy-handed message God wants to give to everyone. To fully understand this second message meant for you and everyone else in this dream interpretation, God had to take me through 40 more years of my life behind the scenes to relive this dream of falling off this cliff; the same way God had to humble Moses for 40 years behind the scenes before God could use him to bring God's message to pharaoh in Egypt and everyone else.

As I started out my life as a new Christian, I wish I understood clearly that God has an enemy—Satan; and because Satan considers God his enemy, Satan considers you and me his enemy too. I didn't realize Satan's ultimate goal in life is to destroy our relationship with Jesus Christ.

He Wants to Separate You from Me

On the night before Christ would be nailed to the cross as the Lamb of God for your sins, my sins and the sins of the world, Jesus was with His disciples upstairs in a large room of a house celebrating the Passover meal. During this "Last Supper", Jesus turned to Peter and said, *"Simon, Simon, listen! Satan has demanded to have you apostles for himself. He wants to separate you from Me as a farmer separates wheat from husks. But I have prayed for you, Simon, that your faith will not fail. So when you recover, strengthen the other disciples."* (Luke 22:31-32 GWT)

Other than the time when Satan tempted Jesus with several requests in the wilderness (Matthew 4:1–11, Mark 1:12–13, Luke 4:1–13), this is the only time in the New Testament of the Bible where Jesus reveals what Satan is asking God for. Of all the things Satan could have asked of Almighty God, he asked to separate Peter and all of the other disciples from *Jesus*. Jesus said Satan wants to *"separate you from Me"*. Of all the things Satan was granted permission to do, it was permission to try and separate all of the disciples from Jesus. Why?

Do you recall another time in the Bible where Satan asked God for a request concerning mankind? It was when Satan asked God to sift Job as wheat to see if he could separate Job from God. The Bible tells us that Job was the richest and greatest man in his region with seven thousand sheep, three thousand camels, five hundred yoke of oxen and five hundred donkeys. (Job 1:3) He was a God-fearing married man with 7 sons and 3 daughters. (Job 1:1–2) Fortunately, we do not have to figure out how the conversation went between Satan and God when Satan asked to sift Job as wheat. The Bible records their conversation as follows:

One day the angels came to present themselves before the LORD, and Satan also came with them. The LORD said to Satan, "Where have you come from?"

Satan answered the LORD, "From roaming throughout the earth, going back and forth on it."

Then the LORD said to Satan, "Have you considered my servant Job? There is no one on earth like him; he is blameless and upright, a man who fears God and shuns evil."

"Does Job fear God for nothing?" Satan replied. "Have You not put a hedge around him and his household and everything he has? You have blessed the work of his hands, so that his flocks and herds are spread throughout the land. But now stretch out

Your hand and strike everything he has, and he will surely curse You to Your face."

The LORD said to Satan, "Very well, then, everything he has is in your power, but on the man himself do not lay a finger."

Then Satan went out from the presence of the LORD.
(Job 1:6 – 11 NIV)

Perhaps what you just read is how a similar conversation between Satan and Jesus went concerning Satan's request to sift Peter and the rest of Jesus' disciples as wheat to see if they would remain faithful to Jesus. Have you ever given it some thought that this is how Satan asks God to sift you and me as wheat to see if we will remain faithful to Christ?

We know a similar conversation must have taken place between Satan and God concerning Peter and the other disciples because Satan said to God concerning Job's relationship with God, *"But now stretch out Your hand and strike everything he has, and he will surely curse You to Your face."* Do you remember what Peter did when Satan struck everything Peter had that night Jesus was betrayed and arrested? Peter denied three times with cursing that he ever knew Jesus right in front of Jesus' face. The Bible tells us that the second time Peter denied Christ, *Peter swore, "A curse on me if I'm lying—I don't know this man [Jesus] you're talking about!"* (Mark 14:71 NKJV, bracketed emphasis mine) When Peter denied Christ the third time in front of the crowd that accused Peter of being one of Jesus' disciples, the Bible tells us Peter was in the courtyard where Jesus was being held when Peter said loudly to the crowd, *"Man, I don't know what you're talking about!" Just as he was speaking, the rooster crowed. The Lord [Jesus] turned and looked straight at Peter.* (Luke 22:60–61 NIV, bracketed emphasis mine) Just as Satan had requested and was grant to sift Job as wheat to see if Job would curse God to His face, Satan requested and was granted by God to sift Peter as wheat to see if Peter would curse God to His face; which Peter did that cold, dark night in front of Jesus' face in that courtyard.

What am I saying? I'm saying that Satan can, has and will ask Jesus to allow him to sift *you* as wheat to test you and see if you will deny Jesus, abandon Jesus or curse Jesus to His face. This is the one card God allows Satan to play.

Have you ever been sifted by Satan? Have you ever felt sifted by Satan? Have you ever denied or refused Jesus; abandoned or run away from Jesus; ever been tempted away from or forgotten Jesus? Have you ever cursed God or Jesus? If you have, Satan was there the whole time.

If you have, this talk we're having is not to condemn you. Just as Jesus forgave Peter for denying Him three times with cursing in front of Jesus' face, Jesus also forgives you for the times you denied Him or fallen away and lived the life of a prodigal son or prodigal daughter. Just come back to Jesus as Peter did and ask for forgiveness; and Jesus will forgive you just as He forgave Peter; just as He forgave me. Jesus is waiting for you at the shores of your return with breakfast on the table just as He did for Peter and the rest of His disciples after they all abandoned Him when He was arrested in the Garden of Gethsemane. (John 21:12)

Satan's desire has not changed today. Of all the things Satan wants to do to you today, it is to sift you as wheat in order to separate you from Jesus. Above all the things Satan is trying to do in your life, separating you from Jesus is his number one goal and priority. Satan knows the best way to steal, kill and destroy you is by separating you from Jesus because your joy, peace, anointing, blessing and protection is with Jesus. That's why Satan asked to sift Job, Peter and the other disciples as wheat; because he knew their joy, peace, anointing, blessing and protection is through remaining and abiding in Jesus. And the way the devil tries to separate you from Jesus today is by trying to separate you from God's word, God's house (church) and His people. Satan knows if he can separate you from any of those things, he can separate you from Jesus.

The original Greek text of Luke 22:31-32 does not say Satan *received permission* to sift Peter or the other disciples as wheat. It only says Satan had *asked permission* to sift Peter and the rest of Jesus' disciples as wheat. However, as we see the way things played out in the Garden of Gethsemane after their Passover meal and the following day leading up to Christ's crucifixion and the days afterward; Satan had indeed been *"granted permission"* to sift Peter and the other disciples like a farmer who separates wheat from husks; and he succeeded . . . temporarily.

Indeed, Satan was not only able to separate Peter and the other disciples from Jesus; he was able to get Peter to deny he even knew Christ three times before the rooster crowed twice that morning following Peter's boast that he would even die for Christ before he would ever deny Him. (Matthew 26:35) Don't forget, Satan knows Scripture better than most of us; and he knows what Scripture has to say about prideful boasting, including these ones that will cause your fall: *"Before his downfall a person's heart is proud, but humility comes before honor."* (Proverbs 18:12 CSB) *"Pride leads to disgrace, but with humility comes wisdom."* (Proverbs 11:2 NLT)

It's one thing when circumstances outside our control separate us from Christ, like those temple guards that dragged Jesus away from His disciples into Satan's den of evil among the religious leaders that night. It's another thing altogether when we choose to separate ourselves from Christ by our own words, thoughts and actions like Peter. Ultimately, it is Satan's goal to get us to do just as Peter did. And he'll use whatever tool of testing and temptation he can from his toolbox of sin to separate us from Christ. Satan has been doing that to people—separating people from Jesus—for centuries and he's gotten really good at it. He's had a lot of practice since the first time he tried it on Adam and Eve.

Has Satan ever been successful with that scheme in your own life?

I have to be honest with you and tell you that Satan has been successful in accomplishing that goal at different times throughout my Christian life. There were many "seasons" throughout my lifetime where Satan had gotten me to separate myself from Jesus or to separate myself from church or a body of believers for one reason or another—it wasn't just a one-time deal for me.

One excuse I used often for not attending church was that I was too busy. During my time in the US Air Force for 20 years, I had to travel for temporary duties and deployments or move to a new state or country every 2 to 5 years. During these moves, I would "forget" to attend church because there was so much to do and see in these new places, cities and new countries. One week away from church turned into one month away from church; and before I knew it, I wasn't attending church anymore. Little did I realize it at the time, Satan was sifting me as wheat with all of those excuses to separate me from Jesus. I didn't realize Satan was keeping me from the power and fruit of a victorious Christian life, and from the protection and blessings that comes with abiding with Christ by keeping me away from God's house and His people. Jesus said, "*I am the Vine; you are the branches. If you remain in Me and I in you, you will bear much fruit; apart from Me you can do nothing.*" (John 15:5 NIV)

Which brings me back to the recurring dreams the Lord gave me about falling over that cliff over and over again to reveal to me how I would fall away from Him, His house and His people—the church—over and over again throughout my Christian life. Just as Jesus forewarned Peter and the rest of the disciples that they would all fall away from Him (Matthew 26:31, Mark 14:27) and forewarned Peter that he would deny Him three times (Matthew 26:34, Mark 14:30, Luke 22:34); the Lord had forewarned me in those multiple dreams when I was 17 years old that I would fall away from Him, His house and His people multiple times later in life.

That was the house I was running away from in my recurring dreams and didn't realize it—I was running away from church, God's house, and I didn't even know it. That's the way Satan would have it— that you didn't know what you are running away from. That way, you won't know what you should be running to—God's house and His people; and you won't see that cliff coming before you fall over.

God in His loving omniscience is constantly trying to warn us of Satan's plots and schemes to sift us like wheat in order to get us to separate ourselves from Jesus and His church. Satan wants each of us to fall away from Jesus and church like someone falling off a high rock cliff or falling from the stronghold of a high fortress on a hill. After all, the Bible says "*the LORD is my rock, my fortress and my deliverer; my God is my rock, in whom I take refuge, my shield and the horn of my salvation, my stronghold."* (Psalm 18:2 NIV)

After Jesus told Peter that Satan had asked to sift him as wheat, knowing full well that Peter would fall away and deny Him, Jesus encouraged Peter with these words: *"But I have prayed for you, Simon, that your faith will not fail. So when you recover, strengthen the other disciples."* (Luke 22:32 GWT) Several Bible versions translate Jesus' words to Peter—*"when you recover"*—different ways such as the following:

"when you have come back to me"
"when you have repented and turned to me again"
"when you are converted"
"when you have returned"
"when you are restored"
"when at last you have come back to your true self"

Which brings me to the second message God has for you and everyone else in the interpretation of my recurring dreams from God—it is the *life lessons of the prodigal son.* I am that prodigal son who has repented, recovered, returned and come home, like Peter, after having separated myself from and abandoned Christ and His church. And like Peter, I've come home to strengthen my brothers and sisters in Christ. I've come home to strengthen and encourage *you.* The truth you're about to read in the following pages of this book will set you free and show you how you should respond to Satan when he tries to sift you as wheat to separate you from Jesus and church; and believe me, he *will* ask Jesus for permission to sift you as wheat. I too am praying for you that your faith will not fail.

It's time now for us to look at the man in the mirror for God's message to you.

CHAPTER THREE

The Dream and the Man in the Mirror

A fool thinks himself to be wise, but a wise man knows himself to be a fool.
William Shakespeare

For now we see only a reflection as in a mirror; then we shall see face to face. Now I know in part; then I shall know fully, even as I am fully known.
1 Corinthians 13:12 NIV

The Man in the Mirror

In 1988, Michael Jackson recorded the song *The Man in the Mirror* that topped the *Billboard Hot 100* charts for two weeks, and later sold over 1.3 million digital copies while becoming the number one single in iTunes downloads in the US and the UK. However, *The Man in the Mirror* hasn't sold anywhere near the numbers that the common everyday mirror has sold.

Have you noticed how a mirror seems almost alive and active? It's amazing how the mirror can bring us both pain and pleasure like no other person can. It can go from being a welcomed friend one day to our worst enemy the next. Since the day it was invented, the mirror never ceases to be a part of our everyday lives from dusk to dawn, from birth to death. While we control it, it seems to control us—how we look and how we dress. It's the first person we see in the morning, and oftentimes the last person we see at night. We've cried before it and we've lied to it. We can't stand it and yet we can't live without it. While we're trying to talk to it, it's talking right back at us. *"Mirror, mirror on the wall, who's the fairest of them all?"*

What you see in the mirror can either help you or hurt you. However, it's not so much what we see in the mirror, but how we respond to what we see in the mirror that can help or hurt us. The mirror itself was never designed to hurt anyone; it was designed as a tool to help us.

It's the same way with this section on the man in the mirror. What you're about to see in this chapter can help you or hurt you depending on how you respond to what you see reflected in these pages. Just as the mirror was never designed or intended to hurt you, the intent of this chapter is not to hurt you—it is designed to be a tool to help you, warn you, encourage you and strengthen you.

God's word is a mirror. It is alive and active as a person—that Person is Christ—who will reveal to you who you really are. Unlike a physical mirror that can only show you how you look outwardly, the mirror of God's word can show you how you really look both outwardly and inwardly; in your heart, your mind, your soul and your spirit. *For the word of God is alive and active. Sharper than any double-edged sword, it penetrates even to dividing soul and spirit, joints and marrow; it judges the thoughts and attitudes of the heart.* (Hebrews 4:12 NIV)

What do you see in the mirror of God's word?

Unfortunately, some people see what they want to see in the mirror versus what the mirror is telling them. How many times have you seen a woman in Spandex only to ask yourself, *"What on earth did she see in the mirror before going out of the house with those things on?"* Sometimes I think God gave men wives to help men see clearly what the mirror is truly telling them before they leave outside that door wearing "those things". Sometimes it helps to have a second opinion on what the mirror is actually telling you. That's what Jesus was to the religious leaders and the rest of the people of His day—He was both the Mirror of God's word and the second opinion about what the Mirror was truly saying about people's lives.

In John 9:39–41, Jesus said to the Pharisees, Sadducees and other religious rulers who trusted in their own righteousness, *"For judgment I have come into this world, so that the blind will see and those who see will become blind."* These religious rulers saw themselves as clean and pure in God's sight when they looked in the mirror. They did not see themselves as prodigal children that needed repentance, forgiveness or a

Savior. They considered themselves the sons of Abraham who did no sin. Therefore, they responded to Jesus, "*What? Are we blind too?*" Jesus responded as a person giving them a second opinion of what the mirror of God's word was really showing them by saying to these religious leaders, "*If you* [acknowledged you] *were* [sinfully] *blind, you would not be guilty of sin; but now that you claim you can see* [your righteousness clearly in God's mirror]*, your guilt remains.*" (John 9:41 NIV, bracketed emphasis mine) Shakespeare put it this way: *A fool thinks himself to be wise, but a wise man knows himself to be a fool.*

Michael Jackson may have wowed us with the song *Man in the Mirror*, but it was Jesus Christ who spoke those words centuries earlier to Pharisees, Sadducees and other religious rulers when He showed them the mirror of God's word and asked them to change their ways. No message could have been any clearer than the words Jesus spoke when He called them hypocrites, blind fools, blind guides, whitewashed tombs (beautiful on the outside but filled on the inside with dead people's bones), full of greed and self-indulgence, snakes and sons of vipers, murderers of prophets and wise men (Matthew 23:13–36 NLT) and children of the devil (John 8:44). Jesus was trying to get these self-righteous religious leaders to take a good look at themselves in the mirror of God's word, and then make a change for the better. But they refused to listen to His words—the very Word of God—or to listen to the lyrics of His song of repentance and turning back to God.

It wasn't just those self-righteous religious leaders that Jesus was trying to get to look honestly in the mirror of God's word. Jesus is also trying to get his people—the church—today to look clearly at the reflection God is showing us when we look squarely into the mirror of God's word. Some people think repentance was something in the past, in the Old Testament with the Ten Commandments; and is not something God is calling us to do today. However, repentance was not something God just talked about in the Old Testament; it was something Jesus emphasized in the New Testament of our Bible too. When Jesus gave the Apostle John the book of Revelation, one of the first things Jesus immediately addressed in Revelation was the need for Christian churches to repent. Notice Jesus was calling Christian *churches* to repent; not *unbelievers* to repent in the beginning of the book of Revelation. Of the 7 churches Jesus addressed in Revelation, He told 5 of those 7 churches to repent from things they were doing wrong. And Jesus didn't try to candy-coat it when He told these churches that they would suffer punishment if they didn't repent.

To the church at Ephesus, Jesus said, "*Remember therefore, from where you have fallen; repent and do the first works, or else I will come to you quickly and remove your lampstand from its place—unless you repent.*" (Revelation 2:5 NKJV)

To the church at Pergamos, Jesus said, "*Repent, or else I will come to you quickly and will fight against them with the sword of My mouth.*" (Revelation 2:16 NKJV)

To the church at Thyatira, Jesus said, "*I gave her time to repent of her sexual immorality, and she did not repent. Indeed I will cast her into a sickbed, and those who commit adultery with her into great tribulation, unless they repent of their deed. I will kill her children with death and all the churches shall know that I am He who searches the minds and hearts. And I will give to each one of you according to your works.*" (Revelation 2:21–23 NKJV)

To the church at Sardis, Jesus said, "*Remember therefore how you have received and heard; hold fast and repent. Therefore if you will not watch, I will come upon you as a thief, and you will not know what hour I will come upon you.*" (Revelation 3:3 NKJV)

To the church at Laodiceans, Jesus said, "*As many as I love, I rebuke and chasten. Therefore be zealous and repent.*" (Revelation 3:19 NKJV)

Jesus describes this generation as One describing what He sees in the mirror by saying, *"How can I describe the people who are living now? They are like children who sit in the marketplace and shout to other children, 'We played music for you, but you didn't dance. We sang a funeral song, but you didn't show any sadness.'"* (Matthew 11:16–17 GWT) In other words, no matter what version of the *Man in the Mirror* song Jesus sang to those who saw what they wanted to see in the mirror, He could not get any response from them. They chose to see what they wanted in the mirror and not to listen to or obey God's "second opinion".

How about us? Are we ready to look at the man in the mirror of God's word? Are we ready to change our ways? Is it time for us to make a change for the better and return back to God's ways, God's house and His people—the church?

If you and I will look honestly and circumspectly into the mirror of God's word, we will discover that *"he is not a Jew who is one outwardly, nor is circumcision that which is outward in the flesh; but he is a Jew who is one inwardly; and circumcision is that of the heart, in the Spirit, not in the letter* [of the law—the Ten Commandments]; *whose praise is not from men but from God."* (Romans 2:28–29 NKJV, bracketed emphasis mine)

Johann Wolfgang von Goethe said, *"Behavior is the mirror in which everyone shows their image."* It's time for us to take a look more closely at the man in the mirror as we view these images of the prodigal son's behavior to determine what reflection we see in these images, and consider what changes are needed in our lives.

A Prodigal Son is a Wasteful Person

The word or name "prodigal" comes from the Latin word *prodigus* meaning wasteful, lavish and prodigal. If you look up prodigal in the dictionary, here are some definitions you'll find:

- Characterized by profuse or wasteful expenditure.

- Recklessly spendthrift (a spendthrift is a person who spends money in an extravagant, irresponsible way).
- Spending money or resources freely and recklessly; wastefully extravagant.
- A person who spends or has spent his or her money or substance in a wasteful, recklessly extravagant way.

By its very definition, a prodigal son is a wasteful son; or more specifically, a person who extravagantly squanders, and recklessly wastes their money, wealth and resources. These definitions sound like something you'd hear in one of Dave's rants on *The Dave Ramsey Show* or on his YouTube videos. By the way, if you haven't already done so, do yourself and your loved ones a huge favor by reading the books *The Total Money Makeover* and *Financial Peace* by Dave Ramsey. These books will show you how live a debt-free life and how to retire as a millionaire without playing the lottery or getting caught up in a pyramid, Ponzi or some other get-rich-quick scheme.

Like so many of us who have read and gone through Dave's Total Money Makeover, I realized how much I had wasted the wealth God put in my hands over the years after reading Dave's book. God put so much money in my hands to invest and prepare for my future years of retirement. Instead I spent it on the pleasures of the here and now. Yes, I too have lived a prodigal life both monetarily and spiritually.

At the same token, God has put so many blessings in our hands for a greater purpose than just our own personal pleasure in life. He intended for us to invest those blessings into the lives of other people. God is waiting for you and me to finish our season and cycle of wastefully living for ourselves and return back home to Him and church where we belong and where we can be a blessing to others. This is where we will find true meaning, purpose and eternal investment not only in this life but in the life to come. When Jesus talked about kingdom investments, He said, *"I assure you that everyone who has given up house or wife or brothers or parents or children, for the sake of the Kingdom of God, will be repaid many times over in this life, and will have eternal life in the world to come."* (Luke 18:29–30 NLT)

If you think about it, Dave's rants about our misuse of money opportunities in our lives sort of parallels Jesus' parable of the prodigal son in Luke 19:12–26. In the parable, Jesus tells the story of a son who asks his father for his inheritance, and then leaves home and goes out and squanders that wealth, leaving himself penniless. This son finally got a good look at himself in the mirror of that muddy swine pit he was in; realized the mistakes he had made and took the humbling journey back home to his father's house to ask his father for his forgiveness, only to find his father waiting there all the time for him, and welcomed and received him back with open loving arms. That's what our heavenly Father wants to do for so many of us who are squandering or have squandered our opportunities. Our heavenly Father wants us to return home to church and to Him and start over again with a clean slate.

People who are prodigal are people who take their time, talents, gifts, and resources and yes, even money that God has given them and waste it on things other than the purposes God intended them to use for the body of Christ and for God's kingdom purposes. It's like we've said to God, *"Thanks pops for what you've given me in life but I've got it from here on out"*, and then we walk out the doors of the church never (or rarely ever) to return there again.

Paul's exhortation about the use of God's gifts in I Corinthians chapter 14 is all about using these gifts for the edification of the church. When God gives us gifts, such as a job and successful career, talents and abilities, resources and opportunities, He give us those blessings not just to help our lives but to help the lives of other people as well.

God called King David a man after His own heart because David listened to and did God's word and will. (Acts 13:22) David gained it all—the entire kingdom of Israel—because he was a man after God's own heart which is the people God cared about. Jesus said, *"Seek first the kingdom of God and His righteousness, and all these things will be added to you."* (Matthew 6:33 ESV) Want to be a man or woman after God's heart today? Then you need to know what God's heart is after.

God's heart is after lost sinners; people who are running away from him and denying Him like Peter; his prodigal sons and daughters. God's heart is after His bride—Jewish believers and God's church. God is also after the widows, orphans, poor, helpless, hopeless and downtrodden in life. David was after all of these too. He was after God's heart by being after God's people when he was willing to give his life for God's house and His people while he faced and fought Goliath the giant and the enemies of Israel. (1 Samuel 17:32, 18:5–6) David was also after God's heart by being after those who were away from God, broke, busted and disgusted; those who wasted their opportunities; the downtrodden who were on the run from people and God—David became their leader too. (1 Samuel 22:2)

David was after God's heart even when he was on the run from King Saul who was trying to kill him. God gave David and his 600 plus fighting men on the run many victories against the enemies of Israel and Judah from which they obtained many spoils of war. What did David do with all these blessings of plunder? Did he keep it to himself? No, David shared them with God's people. He sent presents to cities throughout the nation of Judah and other places where they roamed while hiding from Saul. (1 Samuel 30:21–27) That's a man after God's own heart. That's what God expects of us today—to share what He has given us with His people and for His purposes. I'm not talking about giving online to some charity or putting money in an envelope and mailing it to a ministry. I'm talking about *you*—the talents and gifts God has placed in you—and you giving *yourself* as a living sacrifice by being present in God's house with His people in church, actively involved with them. This, my friend, is a reasonable, holy and pleasing sacrifice to God; one that is after God's own heart. (Romans 12:1)

But there was a time when King David wasted it all as a prodigal king too. Do you remember when that happened? It occurred when David was after his own heart instead of God's heart by taking another man's wife, Bathsheba, the wife of Uriah the Hittite. (2 Samuel 11:1–27) David committed adultery with her. And when she told David she was pregnant with his baby, David tried to cover it up by calling Uriah from the battlefield and getting him drunk so he would have sex with his wife so David could cover his tracks. When that didn't work, David plotted and had Uriah murdered on the battlefield so he could take that man's wife. David wasted God's gifts and anointing on his own life at the cost of another man's life; therefore, God stripped King David of his kingdom—and David was on the run for his life again; this time from his own son Absalom who wanted him dead. (2 Samuel 15:13–14) David lost it all and was back where he started all over again.

Ever been to that place where you know you are back where you started all over again because you made a bad decision or wasted an opportunity in disobedience to God; going your own way, doing your own thing, and now you have to pay the price for it? I've been there many of times on the run from past mistakes like David.

It's all about misplaced priorities. When we seek first the things that are after God's own heart—His kingdom and His righteousness, everything falls into place for us. When we seek first the things after our own heart that are outside of God's word and will for our lives, that's when the wheels start to fall off and we come to a crashing halt in life . . . again. That's when it seems heaven is shut up tight as a drum and we can't seem to get any traction in life or have our prayers answered. The Apostle James put it this way: *"When you ask, you do not receive because you ask with wrong motives, that you may spend what you get on your pleasures."* (James 4:3 NIV) James is telling us that God is withholding what we are asking for because God knows we would waste it because of our prodigal attitude.

Just as we can gain God's blessings in our lives when we seek His Kingdom and His righteousness, we can easily lose those blessings when we stray from God, such as by straying from church. Yes, that's right; we are straying from God when we are straying from church because Jesus and His body—the church—are one. You cannot separate the one (the church) without the Other (Jesus). The Bible says, *"All of you together are Christ's body, and each of you is a part of it."* (1 Corinthians 12:27 NLT) The Apostle Paul asks us this question: *"Do you not know that your bodies are members of Christ?"* (1 Corinthians 6:15 NKJV) In other words, don't you know that when you distance yourself from church—the body and bride of Christ, you are distancing yourself from Jesus himself? Paul hammers this point even further by saying, *"He who is joined to the Lord is one spirit with Him . . . your body is the temple of the Holy Spirit who is in you."* (1 Corinthians 6:17, 19 NKJV)

And what happens when we distance ourselves from Jesus by distancing ourselves from church? The blessings of God fall from our life the way leaves and fruit fall from the branch of a tree that is no longer connected to the tree. Jesus said, *"No branch can bear fruit by itself; it must remain in the vine. Neither can you bear fruit unless you remain in Me. I am the vine; you are the branches. If you remain in me and I in you, you will bear much fruit; apart from me you can do nothing."* (John 15:4–5 NIV)

In Mark 11:12–25, the Bible tells us the story of Jesus cursing the fig tree on the way to the temple. It was no coincidence God chose to set the scene of this story around the fig tree and the Jewish temple (church). As Jesus was headed to church (the temple) with His disciples, he was hungry and saw in the distance a fig tree. So he went over to it *to find out if it had any fruit. When he reached it, he found nothing but leaves, because it was not the season for figs. Then He said to the tree, "May no one ever eat fruit from you again."* (Mark 11:13–14 NIV) The next morning when Jesus and His disciples passed that same fig tree again, *they saw the fig tree withered from the roots.* (Mark 11:20 NIV) Jesus cursed the fig tree for no other reason other than the fact that it was not bearing any fruit. What's the point of this little side story?

If you've been wondering why it seems as if good things are shriveling up, failing or falling off from your life, perhaps it's because you are no longer connected to church or a body of believers which is the body of the Vine—Jesus. And because you are no longer connected to church (the body of Christ), you are no longer connected to Christ. And because you are no longer connected to Christ, you are no longer bearing the fruit God wants you to produce in your life for His kingdom purposes. If we would connect the dots of all the things going wrong in our life or have gone wrong in the past, we might discover it creates a line that points us straight back to a time when we left church or a moment we left a Christian group, activity or fellowship that God wanted us to be a part of. The Bible tells us, *"The LORD will withhold no good thing from those who do what is right."* (Psalm 84:11 NLT)

Every time we stop attending church or stop spending time with Christians that God is trying to connect us with, we cut ourselves off from Jesus the Vine. Every time we cut ourselves off from the Vine, things begin to shrivel up in our life. Our finances start to shrivel up and decrease; our relationships begin to shrivel up and die; our health starts to shrivel up and diminish; our opportunities seem to shrink, shrivel up and vanish; our protection starts to shrivel up and disappear. The reasons these areas of our lives are shriveling up and dying is because God is the source of our finances, relationships, health, opportunities and protection. The further we move away from God's house and His people, the further we move away from Jesus. And the further we move away from Jesus the Vine, the further all of these things—finances, relationships, health, opportunities and protection—move away from us.

On the other hand, the closer we move toward the things that moves God's heart, such as church and other Christians, the more we are seeking God's kingdom and righteousness. And the more we do that, the more all of these other things—finances, relationships, health, opportunities and protection—are added unto us by God. John Gray, the Senior Pastor of the megachurch Redemption Church in Greenville, South Carolina and sought-after speaker at churches, radio and TV shows, including having his own reality TV show, *The Book of John Gray*, on the Oprah Winfrey Network said, *"You want to watch God move on your behalf? Move toward what moves God."*

That's also why Jesus said, *"If you are offering your gift at the alter and there remember that your brother or sister has something against you, leave your gift there in front of the alter. First go and be reconciled to them; then come and offer your gift."* (Matthew 5:23–24 NIV) If you had a falling out with a brother or sister in church, make things right with them first, and then give your worship, gifts and talents to God. Jesus places higher priority on your relationship with your brothers or sisters in Christ than your best worship and gifts to God because Jesus and your brothers and sisters in Christ are "one and the same" in God's eyes. Jesus is trying to tell us that things are not right between us and God when things are not right between us and our Christian brothers and sisters. God views you having a problem with your brother or sister in Christ as no different as you having a problem with *Him*. So why would God want your worship and gifts when you have a problem with Him?

When we are away from Christ by being away from church, not only will we lose God's blessings in our life; we attract problems into our life because devils and trouble are attracted to a soul that is separated from Jesus—they want to go in for the kill. Many of the problems I experienced in life was a result of me running from God when I ran from church—just like that house I was running away from in my recurring dreams. By doing so, problems in my life were running after me, and the attack of the enemy was more prevalent in my life. You can only run so far before you run out of real estate at the cliff and those problems catch up to you and overtake you, just as God said in Deuteronomy 28:15–68 of the Bible.

The reason God does things this way is because God the Father is a good gardener. He knows how to prune live branches that are bearing fruit to help them bear more fruit; and He knows how to cut off dead branches that don't bear any fruit at all. Jesus said, "*I am the true vine, and my Father is the gardener. He cuts off every branch in Me that bears no fruit, while every branch that does bear fruit He prunes so that it will be even more fruitful.*" (John 15:1–2 NIV)

While we are on the run—out on the streets instead of in the seats of God's church with His people, Jesus is pleading to His Father God to give us more time to repent while the Holy Spirit is trying to woo us back to God and back to church. But like the nations of Israel and Judah, God is only going to wait so long before He's had enough of our rebellion and disobedience. In Luke 13:6–9 NASB, Jesus told this parable: "*A man had a fig tree which had been planted in his vineyard; and he came looking for fruit on it and did not find any. And he said to the vineyard-keeper, 'Behold, for three years I have come looking for fruit on this fig tree without finding any. Cut it down! Why does it even use up the ground?' And he answered and said to him, 'Let it alone, sir, for this year too, until I dig around it and put in fertilizer; and if it bears fruit next year, fine; but if not, cut it down.'"* Things will start to stink in your life when God starts adding fertilizer to get you to grow spiritually and bear fruit.

God does not like ruining or wasting soil on a fig tree that is not bearing any fruit because God is not a prodigal, wasteful God. (2 Chronicles 36:21) Do you remember what Jesus said after he fed the five thousand men plus women and children with five loaves and two fish? The Bible tells us *when they had all had enough to eat, He [Jesus] said to His disciples, "Gather the pieces that are left over. Let nothing be wasted."* (John 6:12 NIV, bracketed emphasis mine) Even God likes leftovers. When we live an unfruitful life because we are away from church year after year while Christ pleads on our behalf before His loving heavenly Father; we try God's patience and leave Him no option other than to cut off our blessings and cut us down to size like Nebuchadnezzar by humbling us when we refuse to obey God's word to repent and return to God and His people. Don't become that fig tree that Jesus cursed.

The Prodigal Son is a Disobedient Person

What is a prodigal son? Simply put, a prodigal son is a disobedient son. Perhaps the better question to ask is: "To o**BE**y or not to o**BE**y", if I may borrow the expression from Shakespeare's *Hamlet* because that, my friends, is the real question. Every sin originates from a spirit of disobedience, but before the sin there was always this decision, this question: Do I obey or disobey? That's the question that was facing Adam and Eve before they sinned. Everyone faces this decision to obey or disobey God; and each of us in our own time has chosen to disobey. Romans 3:23 states *"All have sinned and fall short of the glory of God"*.

Sin and disobedience originated with Satan, formerly one of the three chief angels of God (Michael and Gabriel are the other two chief angels), who in his pride disobeyed God and took all that God gave him, and wasted it upon riotous living as a prodigal angel (Isaiah 14:12–17). Satan was the first "prodigal angel". First he drew away one-third of God's angels he was in charge of (Revelation 12:4) to become prodigal angels like himself (Michael and Gabriel are also in charge of one-third of the angels); and then Satan tempted all of mankind to become disobedient prodigal sons and daughters (Genesis 3:1–4, Revelation 12:9).

Satan was once Lucifer, created to be one of the blameless anointed guardian cherubs, an arch angel, who stood before God on the holy mountain in heaven. Lucifer was once a beautiful angel covered in the most dazzling of precious stones in gold settings, but his heart became proud because of his beauty. He was once called Lucifer, which is translated from the Hebrew word *helel* which means brightness, bearer of light or morning star. When he stood before the brightness of God's radiant glory, Lucifer's body, which was covered in so many beautiful precious gems, would reflect the most beautiful and radiant colors that the human eye has never seen. Because of all the beautiful gemstones adorning his body glimmering with so much amazing beauty, colors and brilliance, Satan's pride caused him to become jealous of God's glory and he desired to become a god himself so he too could be worshiped as a god. Satan fell away from God and became a prodigal angel and wasted what God had given him and entrusted to him. Therefore, God stripped Lucifer of his beauty and drove him out of His presence in heaven, and gave him the name Satan which in Hebrew means *adversary*.

The prophet Ezekiel describes Lucifer's fall from heaven this way: "*You* [Satan] *were the seal of perfection, full of wisdom and perfect in beauty. You were in Eden, the garden of God; every precious stone adorned you: carnelian, chrysolite and emerald, topaz, onyx and jasper, lapis lazuli, turquoise and beryl. Your settings and mountings were made of gold; on the day you were created they were prepared* [by God]. *You* [Satan] *were anointed as a guardian cherub, for so I* [God] *ordained you. You were on the holy mount* [heaven] *of God; you walked among the fiery stones. You were blameless in your ways from the day you were created* [by God]. *You were blameless in your ways from the day you were created till wickedness was found in you. Through your widespread trade you were filled with violence, and you sinned* [against God]. *So I* [God] *drove you in disgrace from the mount of God* [heaven], and I [God] *expelled you* [from your glory and position in heaven], *guardian cherub, from among the fiery stones. Your heart became proud on account of your beauty, and you corrupted your wisdom because of your splendor. So I* [God] *threw you to the earth; I* [God] *made a spectacle of you before kings."* (Ezekiel 28:12–17 NIV, bracketed emphasis mine) Now that Satan was fired from his position in heaven and demoted to the earth, he has been trying throughout history to cause the children of God and all mankind on earth to be filled with his same pride; rebel and fall away from God as he did; and become prodigal sons and daughters of God that waste the blessings God has given them.

Satan's fall from his position in heaven was due to his disobedience to God's sovereignty. Adam's and Eve's fall from their relationship with God in the Garden of Eden was due to their disobedience to God's instruction. The fall of the children of Israel in the wilderness when God brought them out of over 400 years of bondage in Egypt was due to their disobedience to God's provision. The fall of Moses in the wilderness when God did not allow him to enter the Promised Land was due to his disobedience to God's holiness. The fall of Jonah when he was thrown overboard and swallowed by a large fish was due to his disobedience to God's call. The fall of Samson when he lost his strength and eyesight after his locks of long hair was cut was due to his disobedience to God's consecration. The fall of Kings David and Solomon who lost their kingdoms was due to their disobedience to God's anointing. The fall of the nations of Israel and Judah and their subsequent captivity in Assyria and Babylon was due to their disobedience to God's law. The fall of all the other nations of the world recorded in the Bible was due to their disobedience to God's existence.

Throughout history, Satan was using deception to cause mankind to be prideful and disobedient. Satan blinds the hearts of mankind by making people think in a carnal, fleshly, natural way instead of thinking and discerning spiritually about the things of God. This is also how Satan deceives mankind into viewing the word of God and the Gospel as foolishness. The Apostle Paul explains Satan's deceptive tactic when he said, *"Satan, who is the god of this world, has blinded the minds of those who don't believe. They are unable to see the glorious light of the Good News."* (2 Corinthians 4:4 NLT)

Jesus tells us about people whom Satan has turned into prideful and disobedient prodigal sons and daughters who will hear the Good News of salvation in Christ but not understand or accept it when He says, *"Though seeing, they do not see; though hearing, they do not hear or understand. In them is fulfilled the prophecy of Isaiah* (Isaiah 6:9): *'You will be ever hearing but never understanding; you will be ever seeing but never perceiving. For this people's heart has become calloused; they hardly hear with their ears, and they have closed their eyes. Otherwise they might see with their eyes, hear with their ears, understand with their hearts and turn, and I would heal them.'"* (Matthew 13:13–15 NIV)

This is why people can be told the truth about the reality of hell but willfully refuse to believe it exists because that would mean we would have to repent of our sins and put our trust in Christ in order to escape the fires of hell. The problem is we don't want to repent of our sins and live godly lives; therefore, we choose to believe that hell is not real. In our made-up minds, if there is no hell, there is no need for a Savior—Christ—to deliver us from hell.

And how will people hear about both the Good News of God's forgiveness of sin in Christ and the bad news of torment in hell for those who reject Christ? Someone has to preach it. And how can anyone preach it unless churches and Christian ministries are teaching and preaching the truth about a heaven to gain in Christ *and* a hell to shun? (Romans 10:14)

And this is where the wheels have fallen off of Christianity in America: Christian churches and ministries in America have also become disobedient and prodigal because they have failed to teach and preach about a hell to shun; they only want to talk about heaven and a loving God without teaching and preaching about a God of severity who will send people to hell if they do not repent of their sins. There's no shortage of people today who want to hear a watered-down Gospel that doesn't mention hell instead of listening to sound doctrine about heaven *and* hell. Satan has successfully caused people to want only to hear sermons that make them feel good. The Apostle Paul wrote to the young preacher Timothy about these types of people by saying, *"The time will come when people will not put up with sound doctrine. Instead, to suit their own desires, they will gather around them a great number of teachers to say what their itching ears want to hear."* (2 Timothy 4:3 NIV)

I know too well this spirit of disobedience in my own life, and so does God. My recurring dreams were God's way of revealing to me beforehand a pattern of disobedience that would reoccur throughout my own spiritual walk with Christ. If life is a class and this world the classroom, then you could say I majored in disobedience to God and minored in obedience. During my Christian life, I was following the pattern of my own recurring dreams—it was a pattern of recurring disobedience. That's why God showed me running from that church house and falling over that cliff each time. It represented each time I fell away from God and church. I realize every one of my falls off that cliff in my recurring dreams when I was 17 years of age was disobedience to God being replayed back to me on repeat mode each night. That's what makes me qualified to write a book about life's lessons of a prodigal son.

The prophet Samuel said, *"Does the LORD delight in burnt offerings and sacrifices as much as in obeying the LORD? To obey is better than sacrifice, and to heed is better than the fat of rams."* (1 Samuel 15:22 NIV) The Good News Translation states that verse this way, *"It is better to obey Him than to sacrifice the best sheep to Him."*

Did you get that? Offering God "the best you have" means nothing compared to simply obeying God. In other words, to obey God is better than your best gifts, your best service and your best worship. Without obedience, nothing you say or do matters to God. Oh I realize what you say and do for God means everything to YOU, but in God's economy, without obedience to God, what you say or do for God is worth nothing.

Just ask Cain. Remember him? He's the guy in Genesis chapter 4 who worshipped and gave God what he thought was his best along with his brother Abel who worshipped and gave God his best too. But the Bible tells us that *the LORD looked with favor on Abel and his offering, but on Cain and his offering God did not look with favor.* (Genesis 4:4

NIV) The NET Bible states this verse this way: "*And the LORD was pleased with Abel and his offering, but with Cain and his offering God was not pleased.*"

Why was that? They both worshipped God. They both gave an offering to God. What was the difference? The difference was *obedience*. Cain was already in a state of disobedience to God when he worshipped and gave to God. Abel, on the other hand, was already in a state of obedience to God when he worshipped and gave to God. It really is just that simple. *Man looks on the outward appearance of things but God looks at the heart.* (I Samuel 16:7) God already knew Cain was evil and disobedient before he gave his offering; and God already knew Abel was obedient before he gave his offering too. This is why the Apostle John tells us, "*Do not be like Cain, who belonged to the evil one and murdered his brother. And why did he murder him? Because his own actions were evil and his brother's were righteous.*" (1 John 3:12 NIV) That's why God was not pleased with Cain's offering. That's why God's not pleased with the best we have to give Him when we are disobedient. If only Cain had looked carefully at the man in the mirror, he could have change his ways before giving his offering. Cain's idea of pleasing God was different from God's idea of what pleases Him. Cain was living out his spiritual life his way instead of God's way. Abel, on the other hand, did things God's way—that was the difference between these two men in the mirror.

Our idea of worship, sacrifice, giving or serving is not necessarily God's idea of worship, sacrifice, giving or serving. God's ways are higher than our ways. In Isaiah 55:9 NIV, God says, "*As the heavens are higher than the earth, so are my ways higher than your ways and my thoughts than your thoughts.*" God desires the kind of worship, sacrifice, giving or serving that comes from His ways and His thoughts. That means God desires the kind of worship, sacrifice, giving or serving that is of His Spirit and of His truth. Jesus said in John 4:23 NIV that "*a time is coming and has now come when the true worshipers will worship the Father in the Spirit and in truth, for they are the kind of worshipers the Father seeks.*" God is not seeking any other type of worship other than the type of worship that is of His Spirit and in His truth. That Spirit and truth is obedience to God's word and His will. In fact, God despises any other form of worship and sacrifice that is other than His true Spirit of obedience. God told the children of Israel who were giving Him lip service but whose hearts were far from Him, "*Your New Moon feasts and your appointed festivals I hate with all my being. They have become a burden to me; I am weary of bearing them.*" (Isaiah 1:14 NIV) It is obedience that pleases God; not worship or giving God sacrifices, gifts or offerings. When our obedience pleases God, everything else we say or do pleases God.

And when you please God, that's when God accepts your worship and blesses you. Proverbs 16:7 NKJV says, "*When a man's ways please the LORD, He makes even his enemies to be at peace with him.*" Put another way, when a man obeys the Lord, God blesses that man to the point where God even makes that man's enemies to be a peace with him. King David said in Psalm 41:11 NKJV, "*By this I know that You are well pleased with me, because my enemy does not triumph over me.*"

What does obedience look like to God? How does one obey God? The answer is simple. Obedience to God is two simple things: Listening to God's voice (His word) for your life and doing it.

It's not enough for us to listen to God's word; we have to do what His word says. Take for example the parable Jesus told in Matthew 21:28–32 of the two sons who heard their father's command to go work in the vineyard. The first son responded to his father's words, "*I will not*", but afterward he regretted it and went and did what his father requested. The second son said to his father, "*I will*", but afterward he did not go and do what he heard from his father. The question Jesus asked the crowd of people he gave this parable to is this: "*Which of the two did the will of his father?*" Jesus said it was the son who said, "*I will not*", but afterward regretted his disobedience and did what his father requested.

The point is clear: It's not the one who *hears* God's voice but the one who follows through and *does* what God's voice says that matters to God. The Apostle James said, "*Don't just listen to God's word. You must do what it says. Otherwise, you are only fooling yourselves.*" (James 1:22 NLT) James continues his discourse about being someone who is a doer of God's word and not just a hearer of God's word by saying, *"Anyone who listens to the word* [of God] *but does not do what it says is like someone who looks at his face in the mirror and, after looking at himself, goes away and immediately forgets what he looks like. But whoever looks intently in the perfect law that gives freedom, and continues in it—not forgetting what they have heard, but doing it—they will be blessed in what they do."* (James 1:23–25 NIV, bracketed emphasis mine) When you look at the man in the mirror of God's word, do you remember what you see God telling you or do you walk away forgetting what you heard from God? That's what I was doing when I would "forget" to attend church when I moved to another state or country every 2 to 5 years while serving in the Air Force. Are we just a hearer of what we see in the mirror of God's word or are we a doer of what we see in the mirror? Are we obedient to God's word and His will for our life? Have we become a prodigal son or prodigal daughter and drifted away from church or are we meeting regularly with God's people? Are we willing to humble ourselves before the Lord and return back to church— His house and His people?

But let's also not fool ourselves by falling into the trap of "righteousness by works of the law" because all our righteousness is as filthy rags the Bible tells us in Romans 3:10. In that old mirror called the Old Covenant explained in the Old Testament of the Bible, it was obedience to the word and will of God based on the Ten Commandments (works of the law) that pleased God. But in the new mirror of the New Covenant of grace in Christ explained in the New Testament of the Bible, the covenant we have with God today, it is now obedience to the word and will of the Spirit of Christ based on faith in Jesus Christ that pleases God today.

So make no mistake about it, the obedience I'm talking about is not some form of self-righteousness we try to work to obtain through following written regulations of the Ten Commandments or any of the other Old Covenant laws. We are made righteous in God's sight only through the shed blood of Jesus Christ. I'm talking about being obedient to the word of God in the New Covenant of grace in Christ and the promptings of the Holy Spirit in our life. The Apostle Paul said, *"Now we serve not under [obedience to] the old code of written regulations, but [under obedience to the promptings] of the Spirit in newness [of life].* (Romans 7:6 AMP, bracketed emphasis mine) If you are struggling with fully understanding this truth about God's New Covenant of grace and obedience to the faith, I highly recommend reading the book *Unmerited Favor* by Joseph Prince, senior pastor of New Creation Church in Singapore.

So what happens when a man disobeys the Lord and his ways are displeasing to the Lord?

First of all, we grieve the very Spirit of Christ that is teaching us the word of God in Christ and prompting us to be obedient to the will of God in Christ when we disobey the Lord. In the words of the Apostle Paul, *"Do not bring sorrow to God's Holy Spirit by the way you live. Remember, He has identified you as His own, guaranteeing that you will be saved on the day of redemption."* (Ephesians 4:30 NLT)

Second of all . . . bad things happen when we disobey the Lord.

The Loving Truth about God's Discipline and Punishment

So what happens when a man disobeys the Lord? God will discipline and punish that person. Just ask the Jews in the Old Testament of your Bible. What happened to the nations of Judah and Israel every time they disobeyed the Lord? Their enemies were at war with them; not at peace with them—and their enemies were winning those wars. In 2 Kings 18:11–12, the Bible records that *"the King of Assyria carried Israel away captive to Assyria . . . because they did not obey the voice of the LORD their God."*

If Ananias and Sapphira were here, they'd tell you bad things happen when you disobey God and grieve the Holy Spirit. You remember that first century couple who died on the spot because they were disobedient and tried to give their offering their way to God, just like

Cain? Peter asked Ananias, *"How is it that Satan has so filled your heart that you have lied to the Holy Spirit and have kept for yourself some of the money you received for the land? Didn't it belong to you before it was sold? And after it was sold, wasn't the money at your disposal? What made you think of doing such a thing? You have not lied just to human beings but to God."* (Acts 5:3–4 NIV)

We often think wrongful behavior that is harming one person or a small handful of people in our lives are not a big deal to God; however, this behavior is actually viewed by God personally as prideful disobedience to Him that God Himself resists and opposes. Take for instance the way husbands treat their wives. The Apostle Peter wrote, *"You husbands must give honor to your wives. Treat your wife with understanding as you live together. She may be weaker than you are, but she is your equal partner in God's gift of new life. Treat her as you should so your prayers will not be hindered."* (1 Peter 3:7 NLT) Just by simply mistreating their wives, God will resist and oppose those husband's prayers as if God Himself was being mistreated by those men. Ladies, this doesn't let you off the hook. This same thing can happen to you and your prayers if you disobey God by disrespecting or dishonoring your husband. (1 Peter 3:1–6) The Bible tells us, *"If I regard iniquity in my heart, the Lord will not hear."* (Psalm 66:18 NKJV)

God expects us to make things right when we've offended someone; not act as if nothing happened. You reconciling your differences with someone you've offended is more important to God than your prayers or offerings or service to God. Jesus said, *"This is how I want you to conduct yourself in these matters. If you enter your place of worship and, about to make an offering, you suddenly remember a grudge a friend has against you, abandon your offering, leave immediately, go to this friend and make things right. Then and only then, come back and work things out with God."* (Matthew 5:23–24 Msg) It's obedience, including obedience in the little things, which brings God's peace back into our lives. More than anything, I need a spirit of obedience. More than anything else, I need to pray for obedience. Without obedience, nothing else really matters to God.

Our problem is not a lack of blessing, favor or opportunity. Our problem is a lack of obedience because God resists and opposes those who are disobedient. I didn't say God resists and opposes those who worship God, who give to God or who serve God. I said God resists and opposes those who disobey Him. Actually I didn't say this, God said this. In James 4:6, God's word says God resists and opposes the proud (the disobedient); but gives grace (undeserved blessings, favor and opportunities) to the humble (the obedient). God will exalt the person or nation who will humble themselves before Him; and He will humble the person or nation who exalts themselves in disobedience to Him—this is all part of God's discipline and punishment. Jesus said, *"Everyone who exalts himself will be humbled, and the one who humbles himself will be exalted."* (Luke 14:11 BSB) The Bible tells us, *"Exaltation comes neither from the east nor from the west nor from the south. But God is the Judge: He puts down one, and exalts another."* (Psalm 75:6–7 NKJV)

The proud think that what they have will last forever, but disobedience causes the proud and disobedient to lose what they have. Without a spirit of obedience, it doesn't matter how great something is that God gives you because you will lose it through disobedience. Just ask Satan. Just ask Moses. Just ask Jonah. Just ask Samson. Just ask King Saul. Just as King David. Just ask the nations of Israel and Judah of the Old Testament of your Bible. Just ask me. Perhaps you only need go so far as to ask yourself if that statement is true.

When the nations of Israel and Judah were disobedient and sinning against God, there were many prophets that God sent throughout Israel and Judah to warn them that they were on a downward spiral further and further from God. The problem was that some of those prophets back then were of God and some of them were false prophets of Satan. The false prophets encouraged their nation to continue in their disobedience and rebellion from God by telling the people and kings of Israel and Judah that *"God is not punishing our nation for our sins"* when bad things happened to their nation. These false prophets blinded the eyes of the people by constantly telling the people that God was on their side even when things looked otherwise—right up to the time when they were taken into captivity to Assyria and Babylon. By then it was too late. They reached the point of no return. So much for the lie that *"God is not punishing your nation for your sins."* The Bible tells us that *Jesus Christ is the same yesterday, today and forever.* (Hebrews 13:8 NLT) If God punished nations for their sins back then, He will punish nations—including our nation—for their sins today and tomorrow.

It's the same way today as our nation continues headlong down that slippery slope of moral degeneracy into more sin, shame, apostasy and separation from Christ—Satan's primary goal. When God tries to get our nation's attention by allowing bad things to happen to and in our nation to wake us up as a nation and bring us back to our senses; we still have ministers—false prophets—today who will constantly tell us that these problems are not God punishing our nation for our sins. These 21st century false prophets of the cloth, these prodigal prophets are blinding the eyes of our nation's people right up to the time God removes all of His protection from our nation. We'll reach the point of no return just as the nations of Israel and Judah did, and we'll find our own nation overrun by our enemies. Let's not wait for that day to happen before we realize that God *is* punishing our nation and people for our sins.

Just before God sent the nation of Judah into a 70-year captivity in Babylon for their sins and refusing to listen to the prophets He sent to warn them about the consequences of their sins, the Bible says, *"And the LORD sent against him* [King Jehoiakim of Judah] *raiding bands of Chaldeans, bands of Syrians, bands of Moabites, and bands of the people of Ammon; He sent them against Judah to destroy it, according to the word of the LORD which He had spoken by His servants the prophets. Surely at the commandment of the LORD this came upon Judah, to remove them from His sight because of the sins of Manasseh, according to all that he had done, and also because of the innocent blood* [killing of children in sacrifices] *that he had shed; for he had filled Jerusalem with innocent blood* [killing of children], *which the LORD would not pardon."* (2 Kings 24:2–4 NKJV, bracketed emphasis mine)

As with King Jehoiakim, what the wicked kings of Israel, wicked kings of Judah and the wicked people of their Jewish nations experienced is one war after another as punishment from God for their sins—one conflict after another; one death after another; one shooting after another; one tragedy after another; one terror after another; and one disaster after another. Sound familiar? It should, because that is what is happening to our nation today for our sins and disobedience to God. So much for those who say, "*God is not punishing our nation for our sins.*"

The Loving Truth about Our Sins and God's Wrath

The Bible tells us that in the End Times, our world as we know it will have reached the point of no return in all of its sin and lawlessness. The Apostle Paul described the evil condition of our world in the Last Days when he said, "*But mark this: There will be terrible times in the Last Days. People will be lovers of themselves, lovers of money, boastful, proud, abusive, disobedient to their parents, ungrateful, unholy, without love, unforgiving, slanderous, without self-control, brutal, not lovers of the good, treacherous, rash, conceited, lovers of pleasure rather than lovers of God—having a form of godliness but denying its power.*" (2 Timothy 3:1–5 NIV) It sounds like Paul is reading the Facebook profile page of America. In case you haven't noticed, our nation is living in that Last Days profile that Paul just described.

During the End Times period, there will be a time of "God's wrath" upon the people of the earth when God will begin killing off mankind for his sins.

Wait a minute, I thought those lying ministers who told you God is only a God of love said nothing about God being a God of anger and wrath? How could there be a time of God's wrath upon mankind if God is a God of love?

Because God is not only a God of love; He is also a holy God of justice, righteousness, severity and wrath. What judge in America or any nation would be worthy of the bench if they did not pronounce judgment and punishment on offenders, including the severity and wrath of the death penalty when it is right and just to do so? No judge would be worthy of being a judge if they let all criminals go free. In fact, we would consider a judge unjust, unrighteous and unworthy to be a judge if he or she could not pronounce judgment and punishment upon someone whose crime deserved it. It's no different with the God of all creation. Because God is a just and righteous Judge, He must pronounce judgment, wrath and punishment on sinners. If God did not judge people fairly and impartially while showing no respect for persons, He could not be worthy of judging the world. That is why the Apostle Paul said, "*Is God unjust who inflicts wrath? (I speak as a man.) Certainly not! For then how will God judge the world?*" (Romans 3:5–6 NKJV)

The Apostle Paul tried to warn us about feel-good preachers that are deceiving people with empty words about God's love without ever mentioning God's wrath or the existence of hell when Paul said, "*Let no one deceive you with empty words, for because of such things God's wrath comes on those who are disobedient.*" (Ephesians 5:6 NIV) Paul warned us that these weak Christian ministers and ministries *by smooth words and flattering speech deceive the hearts of the simple* when they candy-coat the word of God by omitting hell and the wrath of God from their dialog, message, preaching and teaching. (Romans 16:18 NKJV) Even Jesus spoke of God's wrath as He told the crowds about eternal life when He said, "*Whoever believes in the Son [Jesus] has eternal life. Whoever rejects the Son [Jesus] will not see [eternal] life. Instead, the wrath of God remains on him.*" (John 3:36 BSB, bracketed emphasis mine) Jesus is telling us that those who haven't made a decision to put their trust in Christ have already made a decision to reject Him and receive the wrath of God.

Choose Christ today if you haven't already done so.

There are over 600 references to God's divine wrath in the Scriptures, both in the Old Testament and the New Testament of the Bible. In the Old Testament, the Bible describes God's wrath upon the Egyptians that held the Jews in slavery this way: "*He cast on them [the Egyptians] the fierceness of His anger, wrath, indignation, and trouble, by sending angels of destruction among them. He [God] made a path for His anger; He [God] did not spare their soul from death, but gave their life over to the plague, and destroyed [killed] all the firstborn in Egypt."* (Psalm 78:49–51 NKJV, bracketed emphasis mine)

In the New Testament of the Bible, the book of Revelation tells you what God in His wrath will do to all mankind in the End Times who continue in their disobedience, rebellion and sin. *"By these three plagues a third of mankind was killed [by God]—by the fire and the smoke and the brimstone . . . But the rest of mankind who were not killed by these plagues, did not repent of the works of their hands, that they should not worship demons, and idols of gold, silver, brass, stone and wood, which can neither see nor hear nor walk. And they did not repent of their murders or their sorceries or their sexual immorality or their thefts."* (Revelation 9:18, 20–21 NKJV, bracketed emphasis mine)

The Apostle Paul warned people about overlooking the fact that God is both a good and *severe* God, and continue in their sins when he said, *"Because of your stubbornness and your unrepentant heart, you are storing up wrath against yourself for the day of God's wrath [End Times], when His righteous judgment will be revealed. God will repay each person according to what they have done. To those who by persistence in doing good seek glory, honor and immortality, He will give eternal life. But for those who are self-seeking and who reject the truth and follow evil, there will be wrath and anger. There will be trouble and distress for every human being who does evil: first for the Jew, then for the Gentile; but glory, honor and peace for everyone who does good: first for the Jew, then for the Gentile. For God does not show favoritism."* (Romans 2:5–11 NIV, bracketed emphasis mine)

Hello, the Bible just told us God does not play favorites. For those of us who think our nation is God's favorite; and therefore, He will not punish our nation for our sins, we are sadly mistaken. Our nation, like all other nations, must repent and return to the Lord because God is not just a God of love; He's also a God of justice—He does not show favoritism; not for the Jewish nation and not for Gentile nations like America.

Jesus spoke more about God's wrath than He spoke of God's love. Don't just take my word for it; God also has His 21st century prophets that have enough backbone to tell you the truth and are sounding the alarm, like God's truthful prophets of old, to wake us up as a nation. Listen to the teaching and preaching of God's ministers of righteousness who are not afraid to speak the truth about God's goodness and *severity*: Christian ministers and speakers such as Billy Graham, Pat Robertson, John Hagee, David Barton, Jay Sekulow, John MacArthur, Reinhard Bonnke, Francis Chan and Preston Sprinkle.

Read books by authors that aren't weak-kneed, panty-wasted preachers that are more concerned about pleasing people, the status quo and political correctness than God's kingdom. Books such as *The Paradigm* by *New York Times* best-selling author Jonathan Cain, *Trumpocalypse* by bestseller authors Paul McGuire and Troy Anderson or *Erasing Hell* by bestseller authors Francis Chan and Preston Sprinkle. Listen, talking about hell and God's wrath will never be "politically correct" in this fallen world that is deceived by Satan, nor will the subject of hell and God's wrath be acceptable to our prodigal nation. So you might as well put on your man pants and boldly proclaim the truth that God is both loving and severe—by talking about hell and God's wrath— instead of being a lame people-pleaser that only gives people half-truths that don't offend anyone. By trying not to offend anyone, we offended the One who really matters—God!

In his book, *Knowing God*, J.I. Packer wrote, *"God's wrath in the Bible is never the capricious, self-indulgent, irritable, morally ignoble thing that human anger so often is. It is, instead, a right and necessary reaction to objective moral evil."* John Scott, the English Anglican priest considered a leader of the worldwide evangelical movement, wrote in *The Cross of Christ* that, *"The wrath of God is His steady, unrelenting, unremitting, uncompromising antagonism to evil in all its forms and manifestations."* King Solomon, the wisest man in the world, wrote, *"The fear of the LORD is the beginning of knowledge, but fools despise wisdom and instruction."* (Proverbs 1:7 NKJV) If we do not have a healthy fear of God's severity and wrath, we are fools for despising God's wisdom and instruction.

The reason we need to hear about the wrath of God is because His wrath is meant to point us to the cross of Christ. The world in all its wisdom considers the message of the cross to deliver us from God's wrath foolishness. However, God has used the world's disdain for the message of Christ and the cross as a strategic checkmate move in a spiritual game of chess—God has made what the world calls foolishness as the only way the world can be saved from the wrath of God and hell. The Apostle Paul said, *"Since God in His wisdom saw to it that the world would never know Him through human wisdom, He has used our foolish preaching to save those who believe."* (1 Corinthians 1:21 NLT) Our own foolish moves of avoiding the mention of God's wrath and hell that leads us to the cross of Christ on God's chessboard of life will be our undoing that will actually bring upon us and our nation the wrath of God and hell.

When God punishes us for our sins, we won't be able to put the blame on those fake ministers who, like fake news, only tell us half the story—God's love—and omit any mention of God's wrath in punishing sins. Everyone is personally accountable for accepting the truth that God is both a loving God and a wrathful God. We won't be able to say to God that we didn't know about His wrath because all those 21st century false prophets of the cloth told us that God was only a God of love. *If you say, "But we knew nothing about this", does not He [God] who weighs the heart perceive it? Does not He [God] who guards your life know it? Will He [God] not repay everyone according to what they have done?* (Proverbs 24:12 NIV, bracketed emphasis mine) God has told us unapologetically in both the Old and New Testaments of the Bible that He is a God of wrath. In the Old Testament, the Bible says, *"The LORD is a jealous and avenging God; the LORD is avenging and full of wrath. The LORD takes vengeance on His foes and reserves wrath for His enemies."* (Nahum 1:2 BSB) In the New Testament, the Bible says, *"The wrath of God is being revealed from heaven against all the godlessness and wickedness of people, who suppress the truth by their wickedness. For what may be known about God [His goodness and wrath] is plain to them, because God has made it plain to them. For since the creation of the world God's invisible qualities, His eternal power and divine nature, have been clearly seen, being understood from His workmanship, so that men are without excuse.*" (Romans 1:18–20 NIV, bracketed emphasis mine)

In fact, God's wrath increases more intensely in the New Testament of your Bible because God's wrath is poured out in its full force and fury in the book of Revelation. God's message about His wrath has never changed throughout the centuries. What has changed is the spineless message of Christian ministers and ministries in America today who suppress the truth about God's wrath and no longer intelligently and lovingly tell people about God's wrath. (Romans 1:18)

The Apostle Paul was trying to wake people up in his generation when he said, "*So don't think highly of yourself, but fear what could happen. For if God did not spare the original branches* [Jews], *He won't spare you* [Gentiles] *either. Notice how God is both kind and severe. He is severe toward those who disobeyed, but kind to you if you continue to trust in His kindness. But if you stop trusting, you also will be cut off.*" (Romans 11:20–22 NLT, bracketed emphasis mine) The New King James Version of verse 22 says, "*consider the goodness and severity of God.*"

The Loving Truth about God's Severity

Did you get that? God is both kind and "*severe*". The Bible is telling you to consider that God is not only a good God; the Bible wants you to think about and consider the fact that God is a *severe* God! Do not mistake God's kindness and goodness for weakness. God is neither weak nor foolish to where He won't punish sin and disobedience. The Apostle Paul tells us that "*the foolishness of God is wiser than man's wisdom, and the weakness of God is stronger than man's strength.*" (1 Corinthians 1:25 BSB) I make no apologies for saying God is kind, loving and good while being a *severe* God who *punishes sin* at the same time. God Himself wants you to know He is both loving and *severe*. The psalmist spoke of God's character this way: "*Our LORD and our God, You answered their prayers and forgave their sins but when they did wrong, You punished them.*" (Psalm 99:8 CEV)

But notice that our present day prodigal ministers want you to forget about the thought or idea of God being severe; a God who is punishing our nation for our sins. Not only that, the Bible said if you don't consider that God is *severe*, and you stop trusting in Him, *you also will be cut off*. What does it mean to be cut off? Just ask your wife. Better yet, just ask King Ahab.

In 1 Kings chapter 22, wicked King Ahab of Israel was at war with his enemies, and his nation was about to go to battle. Ahab called 400 of his false prophets to tell him if God was on his side before going to battle, and whether or not God would give him and his nation the victory over their enemies. Talk about someone needing a pep talk—it took 400 prodigal prophets to give Ahab a royal *Happy Meal. They all replied, "Yes, go right ahead! The Lord will give the king victory."* . . . *All of Ahab's prophets were prophesying there in front of them. One of them, Zedekiah son of Kenaanah, made some iron horns and proclaimed, "This is what the LORD says: 'With these horns you will gore the Arameans to death!'" All the other prophets agreed. "Yes," they said, "go up to Ramoth-gilead and be victorious, for the LORD will give the king victory!"* (1 Kings 22:6–12 NLT) All of these false prophets where telling King Ahab and his nation that God is a God of love and goodness, and not a God of severity and wrath who would punish him and his nation for their sins.

But what did God's one lone true prophet, Micaiah, say to wicked King Ahab and his nation? *Then Micaiah told him, "In a vision I saw all Israel scattered on the mountains, like sheep without a shepherd. And the LORD said, 'Their master [Ahab] has been killed. Send them home in peace.'"* . . . *Then Micaiah continued, "Listen to what the LORD says! I saw the LORD sitting on His throne with all the armies of heaven around Him, on His right and on His left. And the LORD said, 'Who can entice Ahab to go into battle against Ramoth-gilead so he can be killed?' "There were many suggestions, and finally a spirit approached the LORD and said, 'I can do it!' 'How will you do this?' the LORD asked. And the spirit replied, 'I will go out and inspire all of Ahab's [false] prophets to speak lies.' 'You will succeed,' said the LORD. 'Go ahead and* do it.' *So you see, the LORD has put a lying spirit in the mouths of all your* [false] *prophets. For the LORD has pronounced your doom."* (1 Kings 22:17–23 NLT, bracketed emphasis mine) God's true prophet told King Ahab and his nation that God is a God of severity and wrath who will punish him and his nation for their sins. The prophet Micaiah unapologetically told this Jewish nation that God is a God of wrath.

Both King Ahab and all those false prophets perished in that battle, the same way antichrist and his false prophet will perish in the fiery lake of hell when they go to battle against Christ. The Bible tells us that in the Last Days, *"the beast* [antichrist] *was captured, and with him the false prophet who did mighty miracles on behalf of the beast* [antichrist]— *miracles that deceived all who had accepted the mark of the beast* [antichrist] *and who worshiped his statue. Both the beast* [antichrist] *and his false prophet were thrown alive into the fiery lake of burning sulfur* [hell]."* (Revelation 19:20 NLT, bracketed emphasis mine) These false prophets that perished in hell are no different than our ministers today who are quick to proclaim that God is not punishing our nation for our sins when in fact God *is* punishing our nation for turning our backs on Him. Our 21st century false prophesying ministers have a lying spirit who is telling us that God is not punishing our nation for our corruption, sins and disobedience. These prodigal preachers should beware that they don't find themselves thrown into hell along with all of these other false prophets, the antichrist, Satan and the fallen angels.

Does that mean God will kill people for their sins? Yes, that's what the Bible means when it tells us God is *severe*. The Bible tells us that *"Saul died because he was unfaithful and disobeyed the LORD. He even asked advice from a woman who talked to spirits of the dead, instead of asking the LORD. So the LORD had Saul killed and gave his kingdom to David, the son of Jesse."* (1 Chronicles 10:13–14 CEV)

"But that was just in the Old Testament of the Bible", you say. "I thought God doesn't punish people like that in the New Testament of grace?" you ask."

Don't you remember the true story in the New Testament of the Bible of the 1st century couple, Ananias and Sapphira, who lied to the

Apostle Peter about the money they were giving to the church? The New Testament of your Bible tells us that *God killed them* for lying to the church—both of them fell dead right on the spot they were standing. (Acts 5:1–10) The Apostle Peter said to Ananias, "*How is it that Satan has so filled your heart that you have lied to the Holy Spirit and have kept for yourself some of the money you received for the land?*" . . . *When Ananias heard this, he fell down and died.* (Acts 5:3, 5 NIV) Then Peter said to his wife Sapphira, "*How could you conspire to test the Spirit of the Lord? Listen! The feet of the men who buried your husband are at the door, and they will carry you out also.*" *At that moment she fell down at his feet and died.* (Acts 5:9–10 NIV)

Sounds like God kills people for their sins to me. The Bible couldn't be clearer than that.

Can we please put on our thinking caps for just a minute? Among all the nations on earth from the beginning of time to these Last Days, God could have chosen any nation to be his favorite nation of all the families of the earth to show his extravagant love, goodness and favor. And who did God choose? He chose the children of Israel—the Jews. The Bible makes it emphatically clear that the Jews are God's chosen people in the book of Deuteronomy: "*For you* [the Jews] *are a holy nation to the Lord your God. The Lord your God has chosen you* [the Jews] *out of all the nations on the earth, to be His own. The Lord did not give you* [the Jews] *His love and choose you because you were more people than any of the nations. For the number of your people was less than all nations. But it is because the Lord loves you* [the Jews] *and is keeping the promise He made to your fathers.*" (Deuteronomy 7:6–8 NIV, bracketed emphasis mine)

Now, let me ask you this question: With all that love, goodness and favor that God showered upon the Jews throughout the history of the Bible, did He ever show them His severity for their sins? Yes, numerous times. As you read through the Old Testament of the Bible, it isn't long before you see the severity of God upon His chosen people the Jews in the harshest and most terrifying of ways. Every terrifying curse for disobedience that God spelled out in Deuteronomy 28:15–68, God brought upon the children of Israel—his beloved Jews—with full force when they sinned against Him. God didn't hold anything back. I'll let God tell you for Himself. He said to His chosen nation the Jews, "*You only have I chosen of all the families of the earth; therefore I will punish you for all your sins.*" (Amos 3:2 NIV) That's what I call tough love.

Let me ask you another question: Do you think God flipped the script somewhere midstream in the history of mankind and made America his chosen nation on earth instead of the Jewish nation among all the nations of the earth? Nowhere in the Bible does it say that America is now God's chosen nation. The Bible does say the church—not America—is now "*a chosen generation, a royal priesthood, a holy nation, His* [God's] *own special people.*" (1 Peter 2:9 NKJV, bracketed emphasis mine) So what makes you think God is not going to punish America for our sins if He did not hold back His punishment of His beloved chosen nation on earth—the Jewish nation—for their sins?

The nations of Judah and Israel both came to complete destruction by the hand of the very God who loved them and called them to become a great nation, his chosen people. Why? Because they failed to see and take seriously the *severity* of God along with seeing His goodness and love. By the time these Jewish nations realized they were headed toward complete destruction and captivity, it was too late. Sure they tried calling out to God in the midst of their terror and distress, but by then they had reached the point of no return in their relationship with God. Just as God's word fell on their deaf ears that would not listen to Him; now the tables were turned and they were the ones crying out to God but He refused to listen to their cries. God Himself said, "*Then they will call on Me, but I will not answer; they will seek Me diligently, but they will not find Me. Because they hated knowledge and did not choose the fear of the LORD, they would have none of my counsel and despised my every rebuke. Therefore they shall eat the fruit of their own way, and be filled to the full with their own fancies. For the turning away of the simple will slay them, and the complacency of fools will destroy them, but* whoever listens to Me will dwell safely, and will be secure, without fear of evil."(Proverbs 1:28–33 NKJV)

It's the same way with our nation today—we are headed in the same direction of no return in our relationship with God as the nations of Judah and Israel chose to go with God before their destruction and captivity. God created our nation, loved our nation and made our nation great—just like the Jewish nation. Now we want nothing to do with Him just like those Jewish nations. We're turning our backs on God more and more with each new generation just like those Jewish nations. We choose to listen more and more to the lies of those false prophesying ministers of our day who sing to us that death song: "*God is a loving God; He's not punishing our nation for our sins.*"—just like those false prophets in the days of those Jewish nations. What these *lying spirits* fail to tell you is that God is also a *severe* God who punishes sins and disobedience.

When God is punishing our nation for our sins, do not listen to all of those prodigal preachers who tell you, "*This is not the hand of God punishing your nation for your sins. Yes, go right ahead with your same lifestyles because the Lord is a loving, merciful God who will give you victory.*" Just like Ahab's false prophets, these prodigal ministers have received a lying spirit that are there for the purpose of deceiving our nation further in order to bring our nation to complete apostasy, destruction and doom for our sins. This is why the Bible says, "*We know that God has said He will punish and take revenge. We also know that the Scriptures say the Lord will judge His people. It is a terrifying thing to fall into the hands of the living God.*" (Hebrews 10:30–31 CSB)

Terrifying!

Listen, Freddy Krueger and his nightmares, the dude in the floppy white mask and black hoodie in *Scary Movie*, and scary clowns ain't got nothin' on God when it comes to being terrifying. C.S. Lewis said, "*God is the only comfort, He is also the supreme terror.*" Jesus Himself said, "*Don't be afraid of people. They can kill you, but they cannot harm your soul. Instead, you should fear God who can destroy both your body and your soul in hell.*" (Matthew 10:28 CEV) There's only One person who can send people to the burning fires of hell and keep them there—God! And He's been sending people to hell for millenniums for their sins; He's sending people to hell today for their sins; and He will be sending people to a terrifying place called hell in the future for their sins.

God gives people the free will to choose where they want to spend eternity by accepting or rejecting Christ—that's your part; and based on your choice, God will send you to either heaven or hell—that's God's part. If you have a problem with that, perhaps if I try to explain it this way, it might help you: He's God; you're not—get over it. It's time we opened our eyes to the truth; repent of our sins and accept the grace and forgiveness He freely offers us in Jesus Christ so He doesn't send us to that terrifying lake of fire too. The prophet Isaiah said, *"Seek the LORD while He may be found. Call on Him while He is near. Let wicked people abandon their ways. Let evil people abandon their thoughts. Let them return to the LORD, and He will show compassion to them. Let them return to our God, because He will freely forgive them."* (Isaiah 55:6–7 GWT)

The Loving Truth about Paradise, Heaven and the Kingdom of God

There really is a heaven to gain and a hell to shun. However, faith in God and belief in heaven is diminishing more and more with each new generation in America. The *Religious Landscape Study* by the Pew Research Center, a nonpartisan American fact tank on social issues, public opinion and demographic trends of the US and the world, showed 34% of Baby Boomers (born early to mid-1940s to early 1960s) in America believed in God compared to 28% Generation X (born 1965 to 1983) and only 12% Millennials (born 1984 to 1998) that believe in God. These statistics clearly indicate that America is becoming more godless with each new generation. Imagine what America will be like when all Baby Boomers and Gen Xers are gone and only Millennials, Gen Zers, and the next generations after them are left in America. Do you still think America will be identified as a Christian nation then? Hardly.

The same downward generational trend in America is happening when it comes to belief in heaven. The Pew study showed 72% of Americans believe in heaven compared to 21% who don't believe in heaven and 7% who don't know. Among the American generations that believe in heaven, 32% of Baby Boomers believe in heaven compared to 28% Gen Xers and only 14% Millennials that believe in heaven. Do you see the downward trend with each new generation in America? In other words, Christianity in America is falling over the cliff and dropping further to its demise with each new generation—the same way I fell over that cliff and spiraled further downward each night in my recurring dreams from God.

Paradise and *heaven* oftentimes mean the same thing in the Bible. The main difference between paradise and heaven is that heaven (specifically, the third heaven) always refers to the place where God dwells in heaven. The term heaven is used in the Bible to describe three realms: the first heaven is our immediate atmosphere below outer space under our blue sky where we live on earth and breathe our air; the second heaven is outer space with the sun, moon, stars and galaxies; and the third heaven is the spiritual realm, the place where God, angels and the departed believers in Christ dwell.

Multiple Heavens

The Bible talks about these multiple heavens. For instance, the Apostle Paul refers to multiple heavens when he said, "*Seeing then that we have a great High Priest* [Jesus], *who has passed through the heavens* [plural], *Jesus the Son of God, let us hold fast our confession.*" (Hebrews 4:14 NKJV, bracketed emphasis mine) This is a reference to Jesus passing through the first and second heavens to return to His Father God in the third heaven after He was resurrected from the dead.

Genesis chapter 6 is a case where the first heaven is mentioned when God's patience with mankind had reached its end and He planned to destroy mankind with the Flood. In some Bible translations, such as the English Standard Version (ESV), this chapter describes God's destruction of mankind, animals and birds in the Flood by saying, *So the*

LORD said, "*I will blot out man whom I have created from the face of the land, man and animals and creeping things and birds of the heavens, for I am sorry that I have made them.*" (Genesis 6:7 ESV) In the original Hebrew, that word used for *heavens* in the ESV translation is the Hebrew word *shameh* which means the atmospheric "sky" around earth where birds fly. Another example of the first heaven being mentioned in the Bible is when the Apostle James encourages believers to pray. Many Bible translations, such as the New International Version (NIV), translate James' words of encouragement this way: "*Elijah was a human being, even as we are. He prayed earnestly that it would not rain, and it did not rain on the land for three and a half years. Again he prayed, and the heavens gave rain, and the earth produced its crops.*" (James 5:17–18 NIV) It is obvious that James was referring to our blue sky above earth where rain clouds form—the first heaven—when this translation used the word *heavens.*

Jesus talked about the second heaven when He was describing the celestial chaos that would occur during the Tribulation period in the End Times. Several Bible translations, such as the New King James Version (NKJV), translate that Tribulation period spoken of by Jesus saying, "*Immediately after the tribulation of those days the sun will be darkened, and the moon will not give its light; the stars will fall from heaven, and the powers of the heavens will be shaken.*" (Matthew 24:29 NKJV) This is a clear reference to the celestial bodies in outer space by Jesus when the word *heaven* is used in this passage of Scripture. Another reference to the second heaven in the Bible is when Moses was giving God's commandments to the children of Israel after they came out of bondage in Egypt. Moses warned the newly freed people to not worship the celestial bodies when he said, "*Beware not to lift up your eyes to heaven and see the sun and the moon and the stars, all the host of heaven, and be drawn away and worship them and serve them, those which the LORD your God has allotted to all the peoples under the whole of heaven.*" (Deuteronomy 4:19 NASB) Again, this is a clear reference to the celestial bodies in outer space—the second heaven—when Moses uses the word *heaven.*

The third heaven where God dwells along with angels and believers in Christ who have died is also referred to as the "heaven of heavens" in the Bible (Deuteronomy 10:14, 1 Kings 8:27, 2 Chronicles 2:6). The Apostle Paul specifically mentions the third heaven, the place where God dwells, when he spoke of his vision of being in the third heaven, although he was not certain if he experienced being there in his body or out-of-body when he said, "*I know a man in Christ* [Paul himself] *who fourteen years ago was caught up to the third heaven—whether in the body our out of the body I do not know, God knows. And I know that this man* [Paul] *was caught up into paradise* [the heaven where God dwells]— *whether in the body or out of the body I do not know, God knows—and he* [Paul] *heard things that cannot be told, which man may not utter.*" (2 Corinthians 12:2–4 ESV, bracketed emphasis mine) Paul again refers to the third heaven where Jesus Christ and God the Father dwell when he said, "*Christ did not enter into a holy place* [the Holy of Holies in the Jewish temple on earth] *made with human hands, which was only a copy of the true one in heaven. He* [Jesus] *entered into heaven itself to appear now before God* [the Father] *on our behalf.*" (Hebrews 9:24 NLT, bracketed emphasis mine)

Multiple Paradises

Just as there are multiple heavens described in the Bible, there are multiple paradises described in the Bible too. Paradise can refer to the place in heaven (where God dwells); a place on earth (such as the Garden of Eden during Adam and Eve's time on earth before they sinned); or in "the place of the dead" called Sheol or Hades. *Abraham's bosom* is a reference to the paradise (Luke 16:22) in Sheol (Hades), the place of the dead.

I already mentioned one of these paradises, the paradise or heaven where God dwells, when I quoted the words of the Apostle Paul in 2 Corinthians 12:2–4. When Jesus was giving His revelation to the Apostle John on the Greek island of Patmos, Jesus told John, "*To the one who is victorious, I will give the right to eat from the tree of life, which is in the paradise of God.*" Revelation 2:7 (NIV) When Jesus uses the term *paradise* in the book of Revelation 2:7, this is a reference to the third heaven where God dwells.

After Adam and Eve had eaten the forbidden fruit in the Garden of Eden, they hid themselves in fear of God among the trees of the garden. Some Bible translations retell this story saying, *"They* [Adam and Eve] *heard the sound of the LORD God* [Jesus] *walking in the garden in the cool of the day, and the man* [Adam] *and his wife* [Eve] *hid themselves from the presence of the LORD God* [Jesus] *among the trees of garden."* (Genesis 3:8 NASB, bracketed emphasis mine) The Douay-Rheims Bible (DRB) uses the word *paradise* instead of *garden* when describing the Garden of Eden on earth.

I explain the paradise that is in the "place of the dead" in Sheol (Hades) in the section on *The Loving Truth about Hell.*

Kingdom of God and Kingdom of Heaven

The phrases "kingdom of God" and "kingdom of heaven" are mentioned only in the New Testament of the Bible; however, there is a slightly different use of these two phrases in the New Testament. The only place where the phrase "kingdom of heaven" is used in the Bible is in Matthew's Gospel; however, Matthew also used the "kingdom of God" phrase in his Gospel as well (Matthew 12:28). Mark, Luke and John all use only the "kingdom of God" phrase in their Gospels (Mark 1:15, Luke 8:1, 9:2, 11:20, 17:20, John 3:3); and the Apostle Paul used only the "kingdom of God" phrase (2 Thessalonians 1:5, Acts 28:31, Colossians 4:11, Romans 14:17, 1 Corinthians 4:20, 6:9–10, 15:50). Whenever you read in the Bible where Jesus starts his talk with *"The kingdom of heaven is like . . ."*; this phrase is found only in Matthew's Gospel because Matthew is the only person who uses that phrase.

Whether you are reading about the "kingdom of God" or the "kingdom of heaven" in the Bible, you are reading two different phrases that describe the same thing. Some religious teachers, theologians, translators and Bible publishers may try to strike a difference between these two phrases; however, what matters is how Christ used both of these phrases. Jesus used both "kingdom of God" and "kingdom of heaven" interchangeably when He spoke to the crowds. For example, when Jesus described to the crowds the difficulty rich people have in entering God's kingdom, He said, *"Truly I tell you, it is hard for someone who is rich to enter the kingdom of heaven. Again I tell you, it is easier for a camel to go through the eye of a needle than for someone who is rich to enter the kingdom of God."* (Matthew 19:23–24 NIV) Notice Jesus used both "kingdom of heaven" and "kingdom of God" interchangeably in this passage of Scripture. By the way, the Pew *Religious Landscape Study* confirms what Jesus said about the rich having difficulty entering the kingdom of God (kingdom of heaven). According to the Pew study, the percentage of Americans who believe in God and heaven drops significantly with an increase in income. The study showed that 37% of Americans who make less than $30,000 a year believe in God and heaven compared to 16% Americans making $100,000 or more.

Jesus struck a clear delineation between the kingdom of God (kingdom of heaven) and the kingdoms of man when He said, *"Give to Caesar what belongs to Caesar, and give to God what belongs to God."* (Mark 12:17 NLT) When Jesus was arrested and brought to trial before the Roman governor Pontius Pilate for questioning, Pilate asked Jesus if He was the King of the Jews, to which Jesus replied, *"My kingdom is not of this world. If My kingdom were of this world, My servants would have been fighting, that I might not be delivered over to the Jews. But My kingdom is not from the world."* (John 18:36 ESV) Although Jesus' kingdom—the kingdom of God—is not of this world in which we live, He will return one day to establish His kingdom—the kingdom of God—in this world in the Last Days. The servants or citizens of the kingdom of God (kingdom of heaven) are all believers in Christ and the holy angels who did not rebel with Satan against God.

When God gave King Nebuchadnezzar his frightening dream of the statue's body made of different metals and clay, God was showing Nebuchadnezzar the kingdoms of mankind that would replace his kingdom in Babylon. (Daniel 2:36–43) Lastly in Nebuchadnezzar's dream, God showed him the kingdom of God (kingdom of heaven) that

Jesus Christ will bring to earth to destroy all other kingdoms of men on earth; and establish God's kingdom on earth. The prophet Daniel who interpreted Nebuchadnezzar's dream explained to Nebuchadnezzar that the rock (Christ) he saw in his dream nightmare that was cut out of a mountain (Christ came out of the holy mountain of God in heaven) will destroy the statue (the kingdoms of mankind) in Nebuchadnezzar's dream. Daniel told King Nebuchadnezzar, *"In the time of those kings* [on earth with their successive kingdoms], *the God of heaven will set up* [on earth] *a kingdom* [the kingdom of God] *that will never be destroyed, nor will it be left to another people* [the kingdom of God will not be conquered by another nation]. *It will crush all those kingdoms* [of men on earth] *and bring them to an end, but it* [the kingdom of God now on earth] *will itself endure forever. This is the meaning of the vision of the rock* [Jesus Christ] *cut out of a mountain* [the kingdom of God in heaven], *but not by human hands—a rock* [Christ] *that broke the iron* [Roman empire], *the bronze* [Alexander the Great and Greek empire], *the clay* [mixed with iron is the final End Times government of Satan], *the silver* [Mede and Persian empire] *and the gold* [Nebuchadnezzar's Babylonian empire] *to pieces. The great God has shown the king* [Nebuchadnezzar] *what will take place in the future. The dream is true and its interpretation is trustworthy."* (Daniel 2:44–45 NIV, bracketed emphasis mine)

This is the ultimate goal of the kingdom of God (kingdom of heaven)—to be the only kingdom on earth to rule the earth in the same way the kingdom of God already rules in heaven. This is why we pray that familiar "Lord's Prayer" that Jesus taught us to pray: *"Your kingdom come, Your will be done, on earth as it is in heaven."* (Matthew 6:10 ESV) Whenever you pray that prayer, you're actually praying for the fulfillment of that prophecy God gave through King Nebuchadnezzar's dream of Jesus Christ (the Rock) returning to earth from heaven to destroy all other kingdoms of men on earth in the Last Days, and establish His everlasting kingdom of God on earth to rule mankind forever. When God's kingdom comes here on earth, God's will and ultimate goal for His kingdom will be done here on earth as it is in His heaven. When that day happens, you will be able to call the "kingdom of God" the "kingdom of heaven *and* earth".

In God's kingdom, all control, power and rule belongs to God. Jesus said God's kingdom can also be within you if you believe in Him. (Luke 17:21) In the kingdoms of this world, a limited amount of control, power and rule belongs to Satan because Adam and Eve forfeited all of their limited control, power and rule they had—not what God has—over the earth when they sinned against God in the Garden of Eden. When Satan tried to tempt Christ in the wilderness, the Bible tells us *he [Satan] led Him [Jesus] up [on a high mountain] and showed Him all the kingdoms of the world in a moment of time. And the devil said to Him [Jesus], "I will give You all this domain and its glory; for it has been handed over to me [from Adam and Eve], and I give it to whomever I wish. Therefore if You worship before me, it shall all be Yours."* (Luke 4:5–7 NASB, bracketed emphasis mine) This is how it is possible for empires, nations and people to act wickedly—they are under the influence, power and control of Satan. Even different parties within an empire, nation or regime can act wickedly, just as in our own nation's political parties— Satan is able to blind their hearts and pull their strings like puppets to do his will, instead of God's will, in the earth. This is also the reason why there is so much evil in this world in which we live. It is not because God is not a loving God but because mankind handed over the earth to Satan, making him the god of this world in which we live. The Apostle Paul tells us in 2 Corinthians 4:4 that Satan is the god of this world.

When Jesus returns to the earth in His Second Coming, He will take possession of the earth that He purchased with His blood on the cross, giving Jesus all control, power and rule on earth. Jesus said, *"The time for judging this world has come, when Satan, the ruler of this world, will be cast out."* (John 12:31 NLT) After Jesus paid for control of the earth with his life on the cross, and was resurrected from the dead, He appeared to His disciples and said to them, *"All authority has been given to Me in heaven and on earth."* (Matthew 28:18 NASB) Notice how Jesus said the authority over the earth has now been given to Him after the cross; just as Satan had said earlier to Jesus before the cross that the earth was handed over to him. However, in God's timetable, Jesus will take full possession of the earth when Jesus returns His second time to earth to establish the kingdom of God on earth; and we who believe in Christ will reign on earth with Christ; something His disciples mistimed.

What you see happening in our world today concerning Satan's authority and Christ's authority in the earth can be best understood in light of what happens in America after a new US president is elected. The incumbent US president still operates as president until the end of his term in office while the president-elect has to wait until he can take over the Oval Office. Donald Trump, who won the presidential election in November 2016, was waiting to take over the White House on January 20, 2017. While the then President-elect Trump was waiting for January 2017 to arrive so he could run our country, the outgoing President Obama was still running the country; he still had the power of the president; and was still allowed to make decisions and create policies that affected our country for his remaining 2 months in office.

In the same way, on God's End Times calendar, Satan and his administration of demons has only 2 months left, so to speak, during which he can still exercise a certain amount of authority and control over people on earth whose hearts and minds are loyal to him, as well as things in this world and in this world-system—and he is trying to produce as much damage as possible to mankind and our world before he leaves. That's why the Bible tells us in Revelation *"Woe to the earth and the sea, because the devil has come down to you, having great wrath, knowing that he has only a short time."* (Revelation 12:12 NASB)

The transition of power from President Obama's administration to President Trump's administration was anything but easy. In fact, there is still ongoing friction and turmoil—there is still much fighting going on by the Democratic party, fake news, Obama and Clinton loyalists within government organizations against President Trump, his new administration and the Republican party. It is that same way with the transition of power over the earth from Satan and his kingdom of darkness to Christ and the kingdom of God. That's why Jesus Christ gave the book of Revelation to the Apostle John to pass on to us. God wanted us to know that it's going to take a fight for Christ and the kingdom of God to take back what is rightfully theirs from Satan and his outgoing administration of the antichrist (Satan incarnate), the false prophet, legions of demons and a multitude of deceived people and nations in order to establish God's kingdom on earth. All the chaos and destruction you read about in the book of Revelation are simply the prophetic events that have to happen before the incumbent administration of Satan on the earth is completely removed, and the new administration of Christ and the kingdom of God rules supreme throughout all of heaven and earth.

Satan's days are numbered, praise God! Soon the newly elected King of kings and Lord of lords will come down and move into his new residence at the new White House, so to speak, in the new glorious city of Jerusalem here on earth. Christ may not have won the popular vote among demons and unbelievers on earth, but He won the only vote that matters—the electoral vote of His Father God in heaven. And just as presidents bring their family members with them to the White House when they take over, we who believe in Christ are God's children who will move into this new place of power with Christ to reign with Him on earth when He returns. The policies that Christ will enact on earth will reflect the same policies that are in heaven—God's "will in heaven" will finally be done on earth just as so many of us have prayed in the "Lord's Prayer". The campaign promises Christ made to us before He took office on earth will be the same promises he will completely fulfill after He moves into the "Oval Earth" office.

Would you like to become a citizen of the kingdom of God that will rule and reign with Christ on earth when Christ returns to establish the kingdom of God on earth? The immigration rules for the kingdom of God are different than the immigrations rules for nations of this world. The requirements and cost for getting into the kingdom of God is perfect, sinless righteousness. That requirement is out of our reach for all of us because the Bible tells us that all of us have sinned and fall short of the glory of God. (Romans 3:23) The Bible gives us the profile of people who will not be allowed into the kingdom of God when the Apostle Paul said, *"Do you not know that the unrighteous will not inherit the kingdom of*

God? Do not be deceived. Neither fornicators, nor idolaters, nor adulterers, nor homosexuals, nor sodomites, nor thieves, nor covetous, nor drunkards, nor revilers, nor extortioners will inherit the kingdom of God. And such were some of you." (1 Corinthians 6:9–11 NKJV) Obviously, this laundry list of the unrighteous is not a complete list; but make no mistake about it; you and I are on the complete list of the unrighteous that are not allowed into the kingdom of God because we have all sinned against God. That's the bad news.

The good news is that God Himself has sponsored us to immigrate into the kingdom of God through the payment of the life of His own Son Jesus who paid for our sins on the cross—this allowed God to impute His own perfect, sinless righteousness to us. The Bible tells us that *"all are justified freely by His grace through the redemption that came by Christ Jesus."* (Romans 3:23 NIV) Because of Jesus' blood shed on the cross for us, we now can enter freely across the border of the kingdom of this world into the kingdom of God today; and automatically become a citizen of the kingdom of God immediately without having to fill out paperwork or take tests; work our way into God's kingdom; or wait our turn in line for years to become a citizen of God's kingdom.

Those of us who already made this journey across the border through the Gate of Christ are no longer a foreigner or stranger to the kingdom of God, but rather solid, bonafide citizens of God's country. The Apostle Paul tells those of us who have put our faith in Christ, *"Consequently, you are no longer foreigners and strangers, but fellow citizens with God's people and also members of His household."* (Ephesians 2:19 NIV) Our citizenship in the kingdom of God is not something we can boast about as if we paid for it, worked for it, deserved it or earned it—we were given this citizenship freely by faith in God's grace. Paul tell us, *"Where, then, is boasting? It is excluded. Because of what law? The law that requires works? No, because of the law that requires faith. For we maintain that a person is justified by faith apart from the works of the law."* (Romans 3:27 28 NIV)

Would you like to become a citizen of God's kingdom? Jesus said, *"The time is fulfilled, and the kingdom of God is at hand. Repent, and believe in the Gospel.*" (Mark 1:15 NKJV) If you want to become a citizen of God's kingdom, then pray this prayer with me:

Dear Lord Jesus, I believe You died on the cross for my sins. I confess I am a sinner and I repent of my sins and ask You to forgive me and cleanse me by Your blood You shed for me on the cross. I receive You as my Lord and Savior. Amen.

The Loving Truth about Hell

I know some Christians, pastors and other ministers and ministries like to say, "*God does not send people to hell; you send yourself to hell*", but the fact is you can't send yourself to hell any more than you can keep yourself out of hell. Only God has the power to send people to hell and only God has the power to keep people out of hell. That's why Jesus said to "*fear God who can destroy both your body and your soul in hell.*" (Matthew 10:28 CEV)

The Barna Group, an evangelical Christian research and polling firm, shows only 32 percent of adults in America see hell as "an actual place of torment and suffering where people's souls go after death". The Pew *Religious Landscape Study* showed only 58 percent of Americans believe in hell compared to 34 percent who don't believe in hell and 8 percent who don't know.

Although the existence of hell and God's wrath was widely accepted by the first century church and for many decades within America, it was roughly 30 years ago when people in the US began feeling less restricted and more comfortable about debating the reality and existence of hell and God's wrath. People began speaking and writing books about alternative doctrines to hell, such as political correctness, annihilationism, conditional immortality, universalism, universal reconciliation or existentialism, which over time was digested by American society and became more accepted by the public at large. Individual Christians, ministers and churches in America began following this trend over the past decades by excluding hell from their dialog, sermons and teaching, while other Christian churches and ministries began preaching and teaching alternative ways—besides trusting in Christ—to avoid hell and to get into heaven.

This is simply an age-old tactic Satan has been using for centuries— it's called heresy. Heresy is a belief or opinion that is contrary to orthodox religious (especially Christian) doctrine. Paul and the other apostles had to deal with multiple heresies that Satan constantly tried to introduce into the first century church. Satan tried to inject various heresies into churches of following centuries; and Satan is still trying this old trick today among our generation. Only now, with more advanced technology to reach greater masses, Satan can deceive a greater audience of the hearts and minds of people through the Internet, social media and educational systems to brainwash people into thinking hell does not exist. Another resource to help you understand the truth about the existence of hell is the book *Erasing Hell* by Francis Chan and Preston Sprinkle.

When it comes to hell, it's not about what people say or think; we should listen to what the God who created hell has to say about hell. First, let's define some terms about hell that are sometimes used interchangeably both correctly and incorrectly.

Hades and Sheol – Temporary Hell and Temporary Paradise
The Greek word *Hades* and the Hebrew word *Sheol* is simply referring to the same *place of the dead*—which could be either the place of the righteous dead or the place of the unrighteous dead. Sheol or Hades is supposed to be located somewhere in the heart of the earth (Matthew 12:40, Deuteronomy 32:22, Isaiah 14:9, Ezekiel 31:16). Before Christ died for our sins and rose from the dead, both paradise (the temporary place for the righteous dead) and hell (the temporary place for the unrighteous dead) were both next to each other in that place under the earth called Sheol or Hades away from God's presence. When Jesus was explaining to the crowds about the existence of paradise, which Jesus referred to as "Abraham's Bosom", and hell existing next to each other in Sheol (Hades), Jesus said there was a great chasm (a deep gulf) separating

paradise and hell in Sheol (Hades). (Luke 16:22–26) Although hell and paradise were in the same place—Sheol (Hades)—at one time, hell was the punishing, tormenting side of Sheol (Hades) for unbelieving sinners; and paradise was the peaceful, restful, pleasurable side of Sheol (Hades) for the believers. (Luke 16:22–24)

Prior to Christ's death and resurrection, these righteous dead were given a place of peace, rest and pleasure in the paradise side of Sheol (Hades) but were still separated from the presence of God because the blood of Jesus had not yet cleansed them of their sins because Jesus had not yet died on the cross for their sins. Therefore, they could not be in the presence of God in the paradise in heaven until Christ's shed blood cleansed them of their sins. It was basically a temporary waiting area.

One of the two thieves being crucified on crosses with Christ asked Jesus to remember him when Jesus came into His kingdom. Jesus replied to him, *"Assuredly, I say to you, today you will be with Me in Paradise."* (Luke 23:43 NKJV) This was the peaceful, restful and pleasurable place of the dead in the paradise side of Sheol (Hades) under the earth. That's where this last-minute repentant thief was taken when he died on his cross before Jesus died on His cross afterward.

You can imagine the stir this thief must have caused among all the saints waiting in the paradise side of Sheol (Hades), because he was the first one to announce to all of them that he just came from dying on a cross next to Jesus. (How's that for an icebreaker?) That's when Adam and Eve and their former son Abel, Job, Enoch, Noah, Abraham and Sarah, Isaac and Rebekah, Jacob and his former wives Rachel and Lea, Joseph, Moses, David, Solomon, Daniel, Elijah and all the other prophets and all the saints in the paradise side of Sheol (Hades) must have jumped and shouted with thunderous roars of joy and excitement because they knew at that moment their Redeemer was going to arrive any minute to take them out of that place of the righteous dead in Sheol (Hades) and bring them up to the paradise in heaven to be in the presence of God forever! Talk about being the popular new kid in school. That thief must have made a lot of friends that day—eternal friends, especially with Adam and Eve who got us in this mess in the first place.

After Christ died on the cross at Calvary, paying the full payment for our sins, Jesus went to the expecting righteous dead in the paradise side in Sheol (Hades); preached to the unrighteous dead who were in the hell side of Sheol (1 Peter 3:19); and then Jesus took all those believers in the paradise side of Sheol, including the thief who was on the cross next to Jesus who asked Jesus to remember him, with Him to the paradise in heaven to be in the presence of God because His shed blood now cleansed them and made them righteous and acceptable to be in God's presence forever (Matthew 27:51–53, Ephesians 4:7). Jesus was able to do this for all the saints anxiously awaiting His arrival in the paradise side of Sheol (Hades) because Jesus' death and resurrection now gave Him the keys to Hades (Sheol) and death which mankind previously forfeited over to Satan when Adam and Eve sinned against God by eating the forbidden fruit in the Garden of Eden. In fact, when Jesus reveals Himself to the Apostle John in the book of Revelation, Jesus said of Himself, "*I am He who lives, and was dead, and behold, I am alive forevermore. Amen. And I have the keys of Hades and of Death.*" (Revelation 1:18 NKJV) Jesus is now the rightful owner of Hades (Sheol) and death; Satan no longer has control over Hades and death.

The unrighteous dead remained in the hell part of Sheol (Hades), and are still there today, while the righteous dead in Christ were moved from the paradise side of Sheol (Hades) to the paradise in heaven to be in the presence of God forever. It was Jesus' death and resurrection that allowed not only all the saints who were waiting in the paradise side of Sheol (Hades) to enter heaven; Jesus' obedience to the cross also allowed those 24 elders that are mentioned in Revelation 4:4, some of which also came out of Sheol (Hades), to sit around the throne of God in heaven.

It was Jesus' death and resurrection that made Him the only Person worthy of opening the seven seals on the scroll spoken of in Revelation 5:1–7 that will unleash the four apocalyptic horsemen signaling the beginning of the Tribulation period of the End Times. (Revelation 6:1–8) The book of Revelation tells us that every believer, including those brought out of the paradise side of Sheol up to heaven, rejoiced that Jesus was worthy to open that scroll. They all sang a new song to Jesus saying, "*You are worthy to take the scroll and to break open its seals. For You were killed, and by your sacrificial death You bought for God people from every tribe, language, nation, and race. You have made them a kingdom of priests to serve our God, and they shall rule on earth.*" (Revelation 5:9–10 GNT) The Bible says that "*no one in heaven or on the earth or under the earth was able to open the scroll, or to look at it.*" (Revelations 5:3 NKJV) Those "*under the earth*" who were not worthy to open the scroll or to look at it are those unrighteous souls who are still under the earth in the hell part of Sheol (Hades) today.

So not only is the tomb empty where Christ was laid to rest after His death and resurrection; the paradise side of Sheol (Hades) under the earth is now empty of all the saints who were transported from there to the paradise in heaven in the presence of God. So today, all the righteous dead of the past have been taken and those who will die in Christ now and in the future will be immediately taken to the paradise in heaven to be in the presence of God the Father and our Savior Jesus Christ forever.

Today, any unbelievers who reject Christ and die are still taken to that tormenting hell side of Sheol (Hades) under the earth where they remain temporarily until Judgment Day in the End Times when they will be raised up from the place of the unrighteous dead (hell) to face Christ's judgment in the Last Days. Although I say "temporarily", there are many unrighteous souls that have been in that temporary hell in Sheol (Hades) for centuries suffering in the fires of torment as they wait for Judgment Day where they will have to face their Judge—Jesus Christ—at the Great White Throne of Judgment. (Revelation 20:11–15)

Included in the Who's Who list of people who have been in that temporary hell in Sheol for a long time are the ungodly who perished in the Flood during Noah's time; Pharaoh and the Egyptians during Moses' time; Balaam and Balak who collaborated to cause the children of Israel to sin after they came out of Egypt; people from the cities of Sodom and Gomorrah; Goliath and the Philistines, Amalekites and other ancient enemies of Israel; wicked King Ahab and his wife Jezebel; Julius Caesar, Nero and other Roman emperors; Judas Iscariot who betrayed Jesus; the self-righteous religious leaders of Jesus' day such as the Pharisees,

Sadducees, scribes and Essenes who plotted Christ's death; Attila the Hun; Genghis Khan; Hitler and other murderers of Jews in concentration camps; Ivan the Terrible; Joseph Stalin; Vladimir Lenin; Elizabeth Bathory; and Jack the Ripper.

Are you happy to not see your name on that Who's Who list of hell?

Albert Einstein said, "*The world is a dangerous place, not because of those who do evil, but because of those who look on and do nothing.*" When the 72 disciples whom Jesus sent out to preach the Gospel, heal the sick and cast out demons returned to Jesus with joy announcing that "*even the demons submit to us in Your name*", Jesus told them, "*Do not rejoice that the spirits submit to you, but rejoice that your names are written in heaven* [in the Lamb's Book of Life]." (Luke 10: 17, 20 NIV, bracketed emphasis mine) When you read that Who's Who list of hell, don't sit there snugly rejoicing that your name is not on that list, but rejoice instead over the fact that your name is on that list in the Lamb's Book of Life in heaven because you placed your faith in Christ's death on the cross for your sins—that's what's going to keep you out of hell with the rest of that bunch. (Revelation 20:11–15)

Do you know for sure that your name is written in the Lamb's Book of Life? If not, pray this prayer:

Dear Lord Jesus, I believe You died on the cross for my sins. I confess I am a sinner and I repent of my sins and ask You to forgive me and cleanse me by Your blood You shed for me on the cross. I receive You as my Lord and Savior. Amen.

If you prayed that prayer and meant it, your name is now written in the Lamb's Book of Life.

Gehenna – Permanent Hell
The Greek word *Gehenna* and the Hebrew word *Hinnom* both refer to hell; however, Gehenna more commonly refers to the "permanent" hell

known as the lake of fire. The permanent hell (Gehenna) is not the same place as the temporary hell in Sheol (Hades). In the temporary hell in Sheol (Hades), disembodied souls (spirits of people without their body) of unbelievers are kept in torment among fire as they wait for Judgment Day when they will be judged by Christ. Gehenna (lake of fire) is where both the *body* and *soul* (spirit) of unbelievers will be in torment in a permanent hell of fire after they are judged by Christ on Judgment Day. Those unbelievers who have rejected Christ will experience the full effect of the tormenting fire in both their body and soul (spirit) in the lake of fire (Gehenna). As St. Augustine said in his book *City of God* published in A.D. 426, the bodies and spirits of these condemned unbelievers who are thrown into the lake of fire "*can burn without being consumed, and suffer without dying.*" This is possible because these unbelievers will first be raised from the dead (Revelation 20:13, John 5:28–29, Daniel 12:2); their old bodies will be reattached to their soul (spirit); they will be judged by Christ at the Great White Throne of Judgment (Revelation 20:11–15); and then they—with their resurrected body and soul—will be thrown into the lake of fire (Gehenna) to be tormented day and night throughout all eternity (Matthew 10:28, Mark 9:45). Despite what you've heard or believe, this is the how this true story all of us live, called "life and death", ends for those who reject Christ. For those of you who choose to reject Christ and say, "*It'll all work out in the end*", well this is *how* it all works out for you in the end, the End Times, if you reject Christ.

There are no "second chances" or *Get Out of Hell Free* cards that you will get after you leave this life on earth and find yourself in hell—the temporary hell in Sheol (Hades) or the permanent hell in the lake of fire (Gehenna). Contrary to some popular religious doctrines, thinking and teaching, there is no intermediate place or state after you die—such as purgatory, final purification, final theosis or apocatastasis—where you can expiate, atone for, make amends for, pay indulgences for, experience temporary suffering for, or undergo purification from your sins to qualify you before you are allowed into heaven. The only intermediate place is this temporary hell in Sheol (Hades) before you get sent to the permanent hell in Gehenna. Nothing can qualify you for heaven except the blood of Jesus; and you must trust in Jesus and His blood shed for your sins to cleanse you *before* you die, not *after* you die. Jesus is the only qualified One to expiate, atone for, make amends for, pay for and suffer for your sins so you can go to heaven. To refuse Christ before you die is to refuse your *only Way* into heaven after you die. Neither you nor someone else—other than Christ—can pay for your soul or someone else's soul because a soul is costly; and God doesn't accept Visa, Master Card, American Express, *what's in your wallet*, gift cards, bitcoins, prayers for the dead, indulgences or your other petty bribes. The Bible tells us, "*We can never redeem ourselves; we cannot pay God the price for our lives, because the payment for a human life is too great. What we could pay would never be enough to keep us from the grave, to let us live forever.*" (Psalm 49:7–9 GNT) In other words, God made it an even playing field for everyone who wants to go to heaven. Heaven is not out of reach for any person whether rich or poor, child or elderly, educated or illiterate, popular or forgotten, strong or weak, welcomed or despised, prince or peasant, religious or unreligious. God requires the same payment from every soul to get into heaven, and that payment is only the blood of His Son Jesus Christ.

No one has ever nor will ever be allowed to come out of hell and enter into heaven. After you die, there is only one of two places you will go: you either remain in hell forever or you're allowed into heaven to be with the Lord forever. The only temporary place is the temporary hell in Sheol (Hades) where unbelievers remain until they are brought out of there to be judged by Jesus Christ at the Great While Throne Judgment in the End Times; and then all of them who were in that temporary hell in Sheol (Hades) are transferred to the permanent hell (called the lake of fire or Gehenna) with Satan and all the fallen angels (demons), the antichrist, the false prophet, along with every other person who refused to put their trust in Christ when they were alive on earth. When the people asked Jesus about who would be saved from hell, Jesus told them, "*Make every effort to enter* [heaven] *through the narrow door* [Jesus Christ]. *For many, I tell you, will try to enter* [heaven through other ways besides Christ] *and will not be able. After the Master* [Christ] *of the house gets up and shuts the door* [to heaven], *you will stand outside* [in hell] *knocking and saying, 'Lord, open the door* [to heaven] *for us.' But he* [Christ] *will reply, 'I do not know where you are from.' Then you will say, 'We ate and drank with you, and you taught in our streets.' And he* [Christ] *will answer, "I tell you, I do not know where you are from. Depart from me, all you evildoers.' There will be weeping and gnashing of teeth* [in hell] *when you see Abraham, Isaac, Jacob, and all the prophets in the kingdom of God, but you yourselves are thrown out* [into hell]." (Luke 13:24–28 BSB, bracketed emphasis mine)

The Bible tells us Jesus is the ultimate Judge who will judge all of mankind—you won't be able to appeal to a local, state or Supreme Court judge. Your Teamster union can't represent you; you can't ask for a mulligan; there are no instant replays by the referee; and buying a vowel won't help you solve that puzzle. Only Jesus Christ has the last and final word on where you will spend eternity. Get ready because *"He is coming to judge the earth."* (1 Chronicles 16:33 NKJV)

As Jesus sat on the Mount of Olives with His disciples, they asked Jesus what the End Times would look like. Jesus began explaining to them what this world as we know it would look like when it comes to an end; and then He explained how He would return to earth with an army of angels to judge people—believers and unbelievers—in the End Times. Jesus referred to Himself in the third person when He told his disciples, *"When the Son of Man* [Jesus] *comes in His glory, and all the holy angels with Him, then He* [Jesus] *will sit on the throne of His glory. All the nations* [believers and unbelievers] *will be gathered before Him* [Jesus]*, and He* [Jesus] *will separate them one from another, as a shepherd divides his sheep from the goats. And He* [Jesus] *will set the sheep* [believers in Christ] *on His right hand, but the goats* [unbelievers] *on the left. Then the King* [Jesus] *will say to those on His right hand* [the believers in Christ]*, 'Come, you blessed of My Father, inherit the kingdom prepared for you from the foundation of the world.'"* (Matthew 25:31–34 NKJV, bracketed emphasis mine) Then Jesus explicitly tells His disciples how He will judge unbelievers when He returns by saying, *"Then He* [Jesus] *will also say to those on the left hand* [the unbelievers],

'*Depart from Me, you cursed, into the everlasting fire* [permanent hell called Gehenna] *prepared for the devil and his angels'* . . . *And these* [unbelievers] *will go away into everlasting punishment* [permanent hell], *but the righteous* [believers in Christ] *into eternal life.*" (Matthew 25:41, 46 NKJV, bracketed emphasis mine)

This *"everlasting punishment"* Jesus is referring to is Gehenna, the lake of fire, the permanent hell that you will never be allowed to leave. As I mentioned, the temporary hell in Sheol (Hades) is different from the permanent hell (Gehenna) called the lake of fire. Currently, what most of us think of as hell is the temporary place of torment in Sheol (Hades) where the disembodied souls of unbelievers who have died are sent to temporarily until they are raised up from that place of the dead for the final Judgment Day before Christ (John 5:28–29, Daniel 12:2).

At Judgment Day, books will be opened, including the Lamb's (Jesus') Book of life. (Revelation 20:12) You may not have realized it but God is the best accountant there is—He's kept books from the beginning of earth's creation on every word mankind has spoken, every thought and intent of our mind and heart, and every deed we have done. (Matthew 12:36, Matthew 16:27, 2 Corinthians 5:10, Ecclesiastes 12:14, Romans 2:5–10, Jeremiah 17:10, Revelation 22:12) God keeps such detailed and accurate books about your life that He even records every tear you've ever shed. The psalmist David spoke about God's record books when he said, *"You number my wanderings; put my tear in your bottle; are they not in your book?"* (Psalm 56:8 NKJV)

Those whose names are written in the Lamb's (Jesus') Book of Life are those believers who put their trust in Christ and are welcomed into the kingdom of God. Those whose names are not written in the Lamb's Book of Life are those unbelievers who rejected Christ while on earth and are not allowed into the kingdom of God. After these unbelievers are judged by Christ at the Great White Throne Judgment (Revelation 20:11–15), they will be thrown into the lake of fire—the final, permanent, eternal hell (Gehenna). (Revelation 20:15) The lake of fire (Gehenna) is the final permanent place of punishment for all those—mankind, Satan and the one-third fallen angels, antichrist and the false prophet—who rebelled against and disobeyed God (Revelation 19:20). Lastly, both death and Hades (where the temporary hell is located) are thrown into the lake of fire—the permanent hell called Gehenna (Revelation 20:14). After death is thrown into the lake of fire, no one will ever die again. That curse of death that was brought into this world through Adam's and Eve's sin in the Garden of Eden will no longer exist. (Romans 5:12–14)

The Abyss refers to the bottomless pit that is mentioned several times in the Bible. The Abyss is that same bottomless pit that those legion of demons that had possessed the man in the region of the Gerasenes begged Jesus to not send them into (Luke 8:26–32). After the two witnesses (some believe these two witnesses are Moses and Elijah) in Revelation 11:3 complete their testimony for 42 months (the 3 ½ years of the Tribulation period of the End Times) in Jerusalem, the Bible says the beast (Satan incarnate in the flesh as the antichrist) from the Abyss will attack and kill them (Revelation 11:7, 17:8). This bottomless pit (Abyss) is also the same pit from which scorpion-like locusts will come out of to torment all mankind for five months during the 3 ½-year Tribulation period of the End Times who do not have the seal of God on their foreheads (Revelations 9:1–11). Lastly, the Abyss is that bottomless pit that Satan will be thrown down into by an angel, where he will be bound for 1000 years (Revelation 20:2) while Christ and his bride (the church and the saved Jewish believers) will reign on the earth for 1000 years in God's kingdom on earth. (Revelation 20:6)

Hell is a place of torment, maggots, weeping and gnashing of teeth

The concept of a lake of fire should not be so hard for you to comprehend. All you have to do is look at a fireball lake of lava that flows from an erupting volcano or the hot ball of glowing gases flowing and ebbing from the sun in our solar system. Now imagine yourself in that. And just as the sun's gravitational pull holds all the planets in our solar system captive in its gravitational grasp, hell and the lake of fire will hold the souls of unbelievers captive without ever letting them go. But since our soul (our spirit within our body) is eternal, when someone dies without trusting in Christ, that person will be thrown into the lake of fire on Judgment Day to be tormented and yet not be able to die—they will suffer in that tormenting lake of fire throughout all eternity.

"Death and Hades were cast into the lake of fire [permanent hell]. *This is the second death."* (Revelation 20:14 NKJV, bracketed emphasis mine)

Jesus said, *"As the weeds are pulled up and burned in the fire, so it will be at the end of the age* [End Times]. *The Son of Man* [Jesus] *will send out His angels, and they will weed out of His kingdom everything that causes sin and all who do evil. They will throw them into the blazing furnace* [hell or lake of fire], *where there will be weeping and gnashing of teeth."* (Matthew 13:40–42 NIV, bracketed emphasis mine)

Jesus said, *"Once again, the kingdom of heaven is like a net that was let down into the lake and caught all kinds of fish. When it was full, the fishermen pulled it up on the shore. Then they sat down and collected the good fish* [believers in Christ] *in baskets, but threw the bad* [unbelievers] *away* [into hell]. *This is how it will be at the end of the age* [End Times]. *The* [holy] *angels will come and separate the wicked from the righteous and throw them* [the wicked] *into the blazing furnace* [hell or lake of fire], *where there will be weeping and gnashing of teeth."* (Matthew 13:47–50 NIV, bracketed emphasis mine)

God the Father said, *"But I will tell you what will happen to cowards and to everyone who is unfaithful or dirty-minded or who murders or is sexually immoral or uses witchcraft or worships idols or tells lies. They will be thrown into that lake of fire and burning sulfur* [hell or Gehenna]. *This is the second death."* (Revelation 21:8 CEV, bracketed emphasis mine) It's called second death because the first death is when everyone—the righteous (believers in Christ) and unrighteous (unbelievers)—normally dies the first time here on earth.

Jesus warned the crowd about the terrors of hell when He said, "*If your eye causes you to sin, gouge it out. It's better to enter the Kingdom of God* [paradise or heaven] *with one eye than to have two eyes and be thrown into hell, where the maggots never die and the fire never goes out.*" (Mark 9:47–48 NLT, bracketed emphasis mine)

Hell is a place of punishment and separation from God

Just as heaven or paradise was made as a place of peace, rest and pleasure in the presence of God, hell was made to be a place of pain, punishment and torment while being isolated from God's presence. Heaven and paradise is the reward for those who acknowledged by their faith, words and actions while on earth that they wanted to spend their eternity with God by placing their trust in Christ. Hell is the reward for those who acknowledged by their unbelief, words and actions while on earth that they did not want to spend their eternity with God by refusing to trust in Christ.

The Apostle Paul said of those who do not obey the Gospel of our Lord Jesus, "*They will be punished with everlasting destruction and shut out from the presence of the Lord and from the glory of His might on the day He comes to be glorified in His holy people and to be marveled at among all those who have believed.*" (2 Thessalonians 1:9–10 NIV)

The Apostle Jude said, "*Just as Sodom and Gomorrah and the surrounding cities, which likewise indulged in sexual immorality and pursued unnatural desire, serve as an example by undergoing a punishment of eternal fire* [hell]." (Jude 1:7 ESV, bracketed emphasis mine)

The Apostle Peter said, "*If God did not spare angels when they sinned, but sent them to hell, putting them in chains of darkness to be held for judgment* [Judgment Day]; *if He did not spare the ancient world when He brought the flood on its ungodly people, but protected*

Noah, a preacher of righteousness, and seven others; if He condemned the cities of Sodom and Gomorrah by burning them to ashes, and made them an example of what is going to happen to the ungodly; and if He rescued Lot, a righteous man, who was distressed by the depraved conduct of the lawless (for that righteous man, living among them day after day, was tormented in his righteous soul by the lawless deeds he saw and heard)—if this is so, then the Lord knows how to rescue the godly from trials and to hold the unrighteous for punishment on the day of judgment. [Judgment Day]" (2 Peter 2:4–9 NIV, bracketed emphasis mine) This is the clearest indication from God's word telling believers in Christ that they will not be going through the Tribulation Period in the End Times. We believers in Christ who are alive on earth during the End Times will be raptured and taken up to God in heaven (the third heaven) before God pours out His wrath on the earth meant for unbelievers.

Jesus told us that on Judgment Day, those who rejected Him and God's people while they were living on earth *"will go away to eternal punishment* [in hell], *but the righteous to eternal life."* (Matthew 25:46 NIV, bracketed emphasis mine)

During the Great Tribulation, God will send out three angels to proclaim messages to those still alive on the earth during God's great outpouring of wrath on unbelievers on earth. The third angel will proclaim to the people with a loud voice, *"If anyone worships the beast* [antichrist] *and its image, and receives its mark on his forehead or hand, he too will drink the wine of God's anger, poured undiluted into the cup of His* [God's] *wrath. And he will be tormented in fire and brimstone* [permanent hell] *in the presence of the holy angels and of the Lamb* [Jesus]. *And the smoke of their torment will rise forever and ever. Day and night there will be no rest* [in the lake of fire] *for those who worship the beast and its image, or for anyone who receives the mark of its name."* (Revelation 14:9–11 BSB, bracketed emphasis mine)

Jesus always had harsh words for the self-righteous religious leaders of His day. Without reservation, Jesus would tell them, *"You snakes! You brood of vipers! How will you escape being condemned to hell?"* (Matthew 23:33 NIV) If Jesus was walking on earth today, He would have some harsh words to say to the self-righteous religious leaders of our day who have failed to warn the people of the reality of hell and God's wrath that I just described to you.

The prophet Daniel, whose name means "God is my Judge", was one of the exiles from Judah who was carried away captive to Babylon when God punished the Jewish nation of Judah for their sins. Daniel knew all too well the punishment and wrath of God, having spent his life in captivity in Babylon for his nation's sins against God. Daniel had this to say about God's judgment in these Last Days: *"Many of those whose bodies lie dead and buried will rise up, some to everlasting life and some to shame and everlasting disgrace* [to be condemned to the lake of fire]." (Daniel 12:2 NLT, bracketed emphasis mine)

When Jesus was trying to explain the coming Judgment Day of God to the crowds, He said, *"Indeed, the time is coming when all the dead in their graves will hear the voice of God's Son* [Jesus], *and they will rise again. Those who have done good will rise to experience eternal life, and those who have continued in evil will rise to experience judgment* [of the lake of fire]." (John 5:28–29 NLT, bracketed emphasis mine)

Hell is a place of punishment for Satan and his fallen angels

Hell or the lake of fire was originally created for Satan and the fallen angels (demons); not for mankind. Hell was not originally intended for mankind but mankind decided to join Satan in hell the moment Adam and Eve sinned against God in the Garden of Eden. And this sin of Adam has been passed on to all mankind. (Romans 5:12, 18–19)

Jesus told the crowds that hell was originally a place prepared for Satan and the fallen angels when He said, *"Then the King* [Jesus] *will turn to those on the left* [unbelievers] *and say, 'Away with you, you cursed ones, into the eternal fire* [hell or lake of fire] *prepared for the devil and his demons.* (Matthew 25:41 NLT, bracketed emphasis mine)

The Bible tells us that the permanent hell (lake of fire) is the final permanent place of punishment for Satan when it says, *"And the devil who had deceived them* [unbelievers] *was thrown into the lake of fire and sulfur where the beast* [antichrist] *and the false prophet were, and they will be tormented day and night forever and ever.*" (Revelation 20:15 ESV, bracketed emphasis mine)

The prophet Isaiah spoke of Satan being cast into hell when he prophesied: "*All your* [Satan's] *pomp has been brought down to the grave, along with the noise of your harps; maggots are spread out beneath you and worms cover you. How you have fallen from heaven, morning star* [Lucifer], *son of the dawn! You have been cast down to the earth, you who once laid low the nations! You said in your heart, 'I will ascend to the heavens; I will raise my throne above the stars of God; I will sit enthroned on the mount of assembly, on the utmost heights of Mount Zaphon. I will ascend above the tops of the clouds; I will make myself like the Most High* [God].' *But you are brought down to the realm of the dead, to the depths of the pit* [hell]." (Isaiah 14:11–15 NIV, bracketed emphasis mine)

Although God has not made any provision for Satan and the fallen angels to escape hell, God in His mercy has made a way out of hell for you and me—mankind. God has made a way of escape from being condemned with Satan and the fallen angels in hell by giving His Son Jesus Christ to pay for our sins on the cross. That's why Jesus went through that hellish death of crucifixion on the cross. (Romans 5:18–19) His death had to be hellish because He was paying for our way out of hell. Jesus was paying for our way—the only Way—out of hell and our way—the only Way—into heaven. To refuse Christ today is to refuse your free ticket to heaven and to accept your condemnation to hell.

Have you accepted God's way out through Jesus?

Jesus is your free gift of righteousness from God. Jesus described Himself as being the only Way to heaven in these words: "*I am the way, the truth, and the life. No one comes to* [God] *the Father except through Me.*" (John 14:6 NKJV) Jesus suffered for your sins so you wouldn't have to pay for your sins in hell. Those deep furrows of bone-revealing stripes he took when he was scourged; that crown of thorns that dug deep into his forehead; that old rugged wooden cross and those flesh-piercing nails that were the final instruments of His torturous death; and his agonizingly slow, tormenting, hellish death on that cross before the shouts and scorn of his enemies below Him—it was all for *you* to keep *you* out of hell. The prophet Isaiah describes what Christ did for you and me this way: "*We esteemed Him* [Jesus] *stricken, smitten by God, and afflicted. But He was wounded for our transgressions, He was bruised for our iniquities; the chastisement* [punishment] *for our peace* [with God] *was upon Him* [Jesus], *and by His stripes we are healed.*" Isaiah 53:4–5 NKJV, bracketed emphasis mine)

Hell is a place of punishment for the antichrist and the false prophet

"*The beast* [antichrist] *was captured, and with him the false prophet who did mighty miracles on behalf of the beast* [antichrist]*—miracles that deceived all who had accepted the mark of the beast* [antichrist] *and who worshiped his statue. Both the beast* [antichrist] *and his false prophet were thrown alive into the fiery lake of burning sulfur* [permanent hell]." (Revelation 19:20 NLT, bracketed emphasis mine)

"*And the devil* [Satan] *who had deceived them* [unbelievers] *was thrown into the lake of fire and sulfur* [hell] *where the beast* [antichrist] *and the false prophet were, and they will be tormented day and night forever and ever.*" (Revelation 20:15 ESV, bracketed emphasis mine)

Throughout the Bible, God's word clearly says hell is a very horrifying real place just as heaven is a wonderfully beautiful and real place but unfortunately; very few churches and Christian ministries will teach or preach anything about hell today. That's because churches and Christian ministries today are more concerned about fitting into the status quo of being politically correct so that they don't offend people. These churches and Christian ministries fear that teaching and preaching about hell will decrease the size of their church attendance and media audience which will decrease the money contributions coming into their churches and organizations because of fewer people wanting to come to a church or listen to or watch their Christian program that teaches and preaches about hell. These churches and Christian ministries have chosen the almighty dollar as their God and the size of their members and viewership as their focus of worship by fearing man instead of fearing God by speaking the truth about God's wrath and hell.

Have you ever stopped to think that the reason these survey numbers of people who don't believe in hell have to do with the fact that churches and Christian ministries are no longer teaching and preaching about hell? Solomon, the wisest man in the world, said, *"The accomplices of thieves are their own enemies; they are put under oath and dare not testify. Fear of man will prove to be a snare, but whoever trusts in the LORD is kept safe."* (Proverbs 29:24–25 NIV) Solomon must have been thinking about our present day false prophesying ministers who fail to testify the truth about the realities of hell and God's wrath; who falsely testify that God is not punishing our nation for our sins; they dare not testify about the severity of God and choose not to teach or preach that God will send people to hell if they do not repent of their sins nor put their trust in Christ. As Solomon describes in his proverb, these churches and Christian ministries who are lying to you by failing to testify about hell and God's wrath are accomplices with Satan who is the father of lies (John 8:44) and the thief who comes to steal, kill and destroy your life. (John 10:10) Because these churches and Christian ministries have decided to side with Satan (the thief) by giving false testimonies and half-truths about the severity of God and hell, these false prophesying ministers in these churches and Christian ministries have become an *enemy of their own soul* and the souls of millions of people on earth; they've become their own worst enemy. The fear of man has become a snare to them.

This is in contrast to our Lord Jesus Christ who spoke more about a literal, real hell than any other person in the Bible. In fact, Jesus talked more about hell than He did about heaven in the New Testament of your Bible. Jesus knew hell is so real that He came to this earth to die for us in our place for our sins and disobedience so that we wouldn't have to go to that terrible place. All you have to do is repent of your sins and put your trust in what Jesus did for you on the cross. Jesus knows if you don't accept Him as your Lord and Savior today, He will have to be your Judge at the Great White Throne later and send you to that real place called the lake of fire (permanent hell) on Judgment Day to be tormented forever and ever. The Person who is trying to save you from hell today—Jesus—is the very same Person who will be judging you on Judgment Day tomorrow. Jesus, who is your Savior today, will become your Judge then. What better Person to judge you and send you to hell for your sins than the One who gave His life for you on the cross so that you don't have to go there—that's the ultimate poetic justice for those who choose to believe hell is not a real place. It is this reality about the existence of hell that Christians, churches and ministries need to return to in their dialog, witnessing, teaching and preaching to Americans today.

The Loving Truth about God's Judgment

Despite all you hear about God being a loving God (and He truly is a loving God), He has always judged people in the past; He is always judging people in the present; and God the Father, Jesus Christ the Son of God, and God the Holy Spirit have planned a future "Judgment Day" for all believers at the Judgment Seat of Christ to determine their rewards for their thoughts, words and deeds done for Christ, and a future "Judgment Day" for all unbelievers at the Great White Throne Judgment to determine the severity of their punishment in the lake of fire.

"*It is appointed for man to die once, and after that comes judgment.* [Judgment Day]" (Hebrews 9:27 ESV, bracketed emphasis mine)

The Apostle Paul said, "*We must all stand before Christ to be judged* [on Judgment Day]. *We will each receive whatever we deserve for the good or evil we have done in this earthly body.*" (2 Corinthians 5:10 NLT, bracketed emphasis mine)

The Apostle Peter said, "*God told us to announce clearly to the people that Jesus is the one He has chosen to judge the living and the dead* [on Judgment Day]." (Acts 10:42 CEV, bracketed emphasis mine)

When the Apostle Paul reasoned with the Jews, God-fearing Greeks, all the Athenians and foreigners in Athens, Greece, he said, "*He* [God] *commands everyone everywhere to repent of their sins and turn to Him. For He has set a day* [Judgment Day] *for judging the world with justice by the Man* [Jesus Christ] *He has appointed, and He* [God the Father] *proved to everyone who this is by raising Him* [Jesus] *from the dead.*" (Acts 17:30–31 NLT, bracketed emphasis mine)

"*And this is the message I* [Paul] *proclaim—that the day* [Judgment Day] *is coming when God, through Christ Jesus, will judge everyone's secret life.*" (Romans 2:16 NLT, bracketed emphasis mine)

When the Apostle Paul cautioned us about judging one another, he reminded all of us that we will be judged by Christ in the End Times: "*You, then, why do you judge your brother or sister? Or why do you treat them with contempt? For we will all stand before God's judgment seat* [on Judgment Day]." (Romans 14:10 NIV, bracketed emphasis mine)

When Jesus tried telling the crowds to trust Him now so that He would not have to judge them later, He said, "*There is a Judge* [Jesus] *for the one who rejects Me* [Jesus] *and does not receive My words: The word that I have spoken will judge him on the last day* [Judgment Day]." (John 12:48 BSB, bracketed emphasis mine)

"*Then I saw a great white throne and Him* [Jesus] *who sat on it, from whose face the earth and the heaven fled away. And there was found no place for them. And I saw the dead, small and great, standing before God, and books were opened. And another book was opened, which is the Book of Life* [the Lamb's Book of Life]. *And the dead were judged* [on Judgment Day] *according to their works, by the things which were written in the books. The sea gave up the dead who were in it, and Death and Hades* [temporary hell] *delivered up the dead who were in them. And they were judged* [on Judgment Day], *each one according to his works. Then Death and Hades were cast into the lake of fire. This is the second death. And anyone not found written in the Book of Life* [the Lamb's Book of Life] *was cast into the lake of fire* [permanent hell]." (Revelation 20: 11–15 NKJV, bracketed emphasis mine)

Even the fallen angels will be judged on Judgment Day. The Apostle Jude said, *"I remind you of the [fallen] angels who did not stay within the limits of authority God gave them but left the place where they belonged. God has kept them securely chained in prisons of darkness, waiting for the great day of judgment [Judgment Day]."* (Jude 1:6 NLT, bracketed emphasis mine)

We can try and pretend that we don't hear or see God or don't believe in a hell; that all this talk of Judgment Day and the terrors and torment of hell is just fairy tales made up by the imaginations of men. We can go on with our lives closing our eyes to the truth and laugh in the face of God and His counsel. We can try to comfort ourselves with the words, *"It will all work out in the end"*. God sees another ending for those who refuse to listen to Him. God says in Proverbs 1:24–27 NKJV, *"Because I have called and you refused, I have stretched out My hand and no one regards, because you disdained all My counsel, and would have none of My rebuke, I also will laugh at your calamity; I will mock when your terror comes, when your terror comes like a storm, and your destruction comes like a whirlwind, when distress and anguish come upon you."* This is the ultimate fall off that cliff.

The Loving Truth about the Ones God Hates

Not only is God loving *and* severe, God also loves and hates. More specifically, God loves people and God hates certain people. Before you start telling people I called God a hater, just hear me out. God's word, the Bible, says there are *a time to love and a time to hate.* (Ecclesiastes 3:8) Although we are commanded by Jesus to love one another (John 13:34), the fact is we don't always love everyone. What many people don't realize is that even God doesn't always love everyone. Does that statement surprise you? If you had a problem with God being severe, then you're really going to blow a gasket with the fact that God hates certain people. Sure the Bible says *"God is love"* (1 John 4:8) and that *"God so loved the world . . ."* (John 3:16), but the Bible doesn't say God loves everyone all the time under all circumstances.

Contrary to the popular saying that "*God hates sin; not the sinner*", this is another half-truth that is nowhere in the Bible. The Bible never said that God does *not* hate sinners. However, what the Bible does say numerous times is that God *hates* sinners. Look it up for yourself if you don't believe me. I dare you to find a Bible verse that specifically says, "*God hates sin; not the sinner*". You won't find a verse because it's not in the Bible. Here's what you will find in the Bible:

In Malachi 1:2–3 GWT, God said, "*I loved Jacob, but **Esau I hated**, and made his mountains a desolation, and gave his heritage to the jackals of the wilderness.*" Just to make sure you didn't think that was a misprint in the Old Testament or that this was something God said only in the Old Testament but not in the New Testament of the Bible, God repeats His words again in the New Testament: "*Jacob I loved, but **Esau I hated**.*" (Romans 9:13 NIV)

Psalm 5:4–5 ESV describes God this way: "*You are not a God who delights in wickedness; evil may not dwell with You. The boastful shall not stand before Your eyes; **You hate all evildoers**.*"

When God was giving his commandments to the children of Israel in the wilderness after they came out of bondage in Egypt, God told them, "*You must not live according to the customs of the nations I am going to drive out before you. Because they did all these* [evil] *things, **I abhorred them**.*" (Leviticus 20:23 NIV, bracketed emphasis mine) Do you know what the word "abhorred" means? It means to regard with disgust and hatred. To abhor someone is to detest, hate, loathe and despise that person. In other words, God doesn't just hate people who do evil; he detests, loathes and despises them.

Psalm 5:6 NLT describes God's character this way: "*You will destroy those who tell lies. **The LORD detests murderers and deceivers**.*"

Psalm 11:5 NIV says, *"The LORD examines the righteous, but* ***the
wicked, those who love violence, He hates with a passion."*** To
hate someone is one thing, but to hate them with a passion takes it to a
whole nother level. (I realize "nother" is not a word—get over it.)

The book of Proverbs goes so far as to give you a list of the type of
people the Lord hates: ***"There are six things which the LORD
hates, yes, seven which are an abomination to Him***: *haughty
eyes, a lying tongue, and hands that shed innocent blood, a heart that
devise wicked plans, feet that run rapidly to evil, a false witness who
utters lies, and one who spreads strife among brothers."* (Proverbs
6:16– 9 NASB) If you do any of those things, guess what? God hates you.

And what do you suppose God thinks of you when you choose to
continue to sin and rebel against His word and will for your life to return
to Him, His house and His people? (Zechariah 1:3, Hebrews 10:25)

If it looks like a duck, smells like a duck and walks like a duck, it's a
duck—you can cook it and eat it. If it looks like crap, smells like crap and
sits there like carp, it is crap—why would you want to eat it? And yet,
people are eating this crap about *"God hates the sin, not the sinner"* or
"hell is not a real place of torment" or *"God is too loving to send people
to hell because of their sins".* Hell is a real place and you know who God
sends to hell? People He hates. And who does God hate? God hates
unbelieving, wicked, sinful, disobedient people.

Where do you think we got the ability and capacity to love people
and hate people? The ability to hate people did not come from Satan or
through Adam's and Eve's fall in the Garden of Eden. We were made in
the image of God who has the ability and capacity to both love people and
hate people. The reason it's possible for us to love and hate people is
because God can love and hate people. When the nation of Israel had
stretched God's patience to the breaking point with their sins and
disobedience, God sent them the prophet Hosea to tell them these words:

*The LORD says, "All their wickedness began at Gilgal; there **I** **began to hate them**. I will drive them from my land because of their evil actions. **I will love them no more** because all their leaders are rebels."* (Hosea 9:15 NLT)

So where did the statement *"God hates sin; not the sinner"* or *"hate the sin but not the sinner"* come from? It came from a letter written in A.D. 423 by St. Augustine, a Roman African bishop of the ancient city of Hippo in Africa, that contained the Latin phrase *"Cum dilectione hominum et odio vitiorum"* which means *"With love for mankind and hatred of sins"*. Over the years, individuals and churches have borrowed and modified St. Augustine's words to say *"God hates sin; not the sinner"* or *"hate the sin but not the sinner"*. Today, people think St. Augustine's words are Gospel which they are not.

God knows how hatred can destroy another person's life, such as Cain who destroyed his brother Abel's life because of his hatred for Abel; or Joseph's brothers who sold him into slavery because of their hatred for Joseph. God also knows hatred can destroy you and your own life like Jonah whose life was swallowed up by a great fish because of his hatred for the people of Nineveh; or Moses' sister Miriam whom God punished with leprosy because she hated Moses' wife who was a Cushite, a Black African woman from Ethiopia who had dark complexion. That's why God tells us to love our enemies (Matthew 5:44) just as God so loved the world filled with His enemies (John 3:16); to forgive those who offend us (Colossians 3:13) just as Christ forgave our sins (Ephesians 4:32); and to cover the sins of others with love (1 Peter 4:8).

That's what God had to do for you and me. Instead of choosing to hate us because of our sins, God chose to forgive all of our sins by giving His own Son Jesus to die for our sins. You see, God is a God of justice, righteousness and holiness who must judge sins—that means someone has to pay the penalty for our sins. But God so loved the world—that means you and me—that He gave His only Son Jesus on our behalf to die for our sins so that whosoever—that means you and me—believes in Jesus will not perish in hell with the people God hates, but will have everlasting life. (John 3:16) Instead of sending us into captivity in hell for our sins the way God sent the nations of Israel and Judah into captivity for their sins, God chose to administer our punishment upon His own Son by giving up His only beloved Son Jesus in our place. God gave you His Son's righteousness and gave His Son your sins—a Divine exchange that removes the wrath of God from your life if you simply trust in His grace (undeserved favor) given to you in Jesus Christ. The Bible tells us that "*He* [God the Father] *made Him* [Jesus] *who knew no sin to be sin for us, that we might become the righteousness of God in Him* [Jesus]." (2 Corinthians 5:21 NKJV, bracketed emphasis mine) The Apostle Paul tells us that just "*by one man's* [Adam's] *disobedience many* [that means you and me] *were made sinners, so also by one Man's* [Jesus'] *obedience many* [that means you and me] *will be made righteous.*" (Romans 5:19 NKJV, bracketed emphasis mine) That's God's severity, hatred, justice, righteousness, holiness, love, goodness, mercy and grace operating in unison and agreement with each other to clear you and cleanse you of all guilt of sin. That's the power of God's grace and the power of the Gospel (Good News) about Jesus Christ; but you can't comprehend and appreciate the Good News of God's grace unless you first understand and accept the bad news of hell.

The Prodigal Son Doesn't Think He Needs a Savior

Listen, I'm in agreement with teachers and preachers who emphasize "faith" in the *abundance of God's grace* and His *gift of righteousness* to the world. (Romans 5:17) I think our world needs to hear more of that Gospel (Good News) about God freely offering us His abundance of grace to forgive us of all our sins and His gift of righteousness given to us through our Lord and Savior Jesus Christ to make us holy and acceptable in His sight. But what these teachers and preachers of faith do not realize is that people are not going to want God's abundance of grace nor His gift of righteousness if they don't see a need for it. And they don't see their need for God's abundant grace and gift of righteousness because *they don't believe there is a hell!* Since they believe there is no hell, they believe there is no need for a Savior from hell. It's that simple. It's the same thing if you don't believe your house is on fire, you don't believe you need firemen to save your house. Therefore, we must emphasize hell so that people can understand and appreciate their need for God's abundance of grace and His gift of righteousness through our Savior Jesus Christ to rescue us from hell.

Let me ask you a question: If you are enjoying a swim in a public pool with other people; and the lifeguard throws a life preserver ring at you and yells, *"Grab hold of it, it'll save you"*, would you grab onto it like it meant life or death for you to use that floatation device? Of course you wouldn't. You would look at that lifeguard like he or she was crazy. In fact, you would get upset and probably leave that pool and never come back there again because you didn't think you were drowning. And yet, that lifeguard insulted you by thinking you couldn't swim and needed saving. You would say, *"There's nothing wrong with the way I'm swimming. I'm not drowning. I don't need to be saved."*

It's no different when churches do not educate people about God's wrath and the existence of hell. People think they are swimming along fine in life not knowing or believing they are going to drown in the lake of fire because they don't believe in the wrath of God or the existence of hell. When you offer them God's life preserver ring—Jesus Christ—they look at you like you're crazy because they don't believe they need saving from anything. King Solomon, the wisest man in the world said, *"By the fear of the LORD one departs from evil."* (Proverbs 16:6 NKJV)

Just like the person in the pool, people are leaving church angry and upset not because the church is teaching and preaching about the wrath of God or hell (because churches are no longer talking about God's wrath and hell). Just the opposite is happening. People are leaving the church angry and upset because the church is *not* educating them about the wrath of God and hell. That's the missing piece that is causing more and more people to get out of the pool and leave church today—they simply to do not see a need for a Savior Jesus Christ, the church or God's abundance of grace and His gift of righteousness because they believe there is no wrath of God or hell to fear. And because they believe there is no wrath of God or hell, in their minds they're saying, *"There's nothing wrong with the way I'm living. I'm not drowning in the lake of fire. I don't need to be saved."*

You don't have to believe me; just look at the dwindling numbers of people attending churches in America and the undeniable, statistical fact that church attendance in America is decreasing—not increasing—each year. As the old saying goes, *the definition of insanity is doing the same thing over and over again, expecting a different result.* Churches have been neglecting the wrath of God and hell in their preaching and teaching over the past 30 years, expecting a different result of people returning to church, but just the opposite is happening in America each year. It's time Christianity in America woke up to the statistical fact that omitting the preaching and teaching of God's wrath and hell over the past decades is a failed experiment—it has not helped to increase church attendance; it drastically decreased church attendance over the past 30 years.

Sure, the Bible says, *"How beautiful are the feet of those who preach the gospel of peace, who bring glad tidings of good things."* (Romans 10:15 NKJV) But those feet aren't attractive at all to a person who believes the Gospel is irrelevant because they don't believe in God's wrath or hell. Those are unnecessary tidings about irrelevant things to someone who doesn't believe God's wrath or hell exists. Just two verses after Romans 10:15, the Bible also says that *"faith comes from hearing, and hearing [comes] through the word of Christ."* (Romans 10:17 ESV, bracketed emphasis mine) Did you hear that? Faith comes from the word, the message of Christ. The message Christ spoke included hell—a lot about hell. That's what produces faith along with the Good News of salvation from God's wrath and hell.

Post-Christianity in America – The New Prodigal Nation

The Barna Group gives us plenty of data showing how Americans are becoming more "post-Christian" than ever before. A post-Christian person is someone who no longer fits the profile of the Christian identity, belief and practice. This growing group of post-Christians in America include people who do not believe in God or claim to be atheist or agnostic; don't read the Bible or don't believe it is accurate; have no faith in Christ or believe Christ may have sinned; do not pray, share their faith, attend a Christian church or other church activities, nor give money to church or Christian charities.

Barna statistics clearly show that each new generation in America has become more post-Christian than the previous generation. This is in line with an already known fact that children rarely rise to a higher standard of moral conduct than that of their parents. Barna tells us that our Generation Z (born between 1999 and 2015) is the first post-Christian generation in America, having more post-Christians in this generation than any other previous generation, and double the number of atheists than the number of adults in the entire American population.

When Barna asked non-Christians in all generational groups— Generation Z, Millennials (born 1984 to 1998), Generation X (born 1965 to 1983) and Baby Boomers (born early to mid-1940s to early 1960s)— what was their biggest barriers to embracing the Christian faith, the Gen Zers and Millennials stated more so than Gen Xers and Baby Boomers that their biggest hindrance to accepting the Christian faith is they have not found a *"compelling argument for the existence of both evil and a good and loving God"*.

Hey Christianity in America, are you listening to that response from post-Christians in America?! The reason the numbers of church attendance and involvement with Christianity in America continue to drop so drastically each year is because Christians, churches and ministries have not given our nation's people the truth, compelling truth about the existence of evil in this world and how a good and loving God can stand by watching all this evil happening without doing anything about it. This is straight from the mouths of post-Christian people that you want to return to your Christian faith and churches in America!

The reason our nation's people have not heard a compelling argument about how a good and loving God can allow all this evil in our world to exist is because no one has told them God *is* doing something about all the evil—that *something* is called the wrath of God and hell. The

Bible clearly states that *"because of your stubbornness and your unrepentant heart, you are storing up wrath against yourself for the day of God's wrath, when His righteous judgment will be revealed. God will repay each person according to what they have done. To those who by persistence in doing good seek glory, honor and immortality, He will give eternal life. But for those who are self-seeking and who reject the truth and follow evil, there will be wrath and anger. There will be trouble and distress for every human being who does evil: first for the Jew, then for the Gentile; but glory, honor and peace for everyone who does good: first for the Jew, then for the Gentile. For God does not show favoritism."* (Romans 2:5–11 NIV)

But Christian churches and ministries in America today have chosen not to mention the wrath of God and hell anymore; therefore, our people do not see the justice and power of God in dealing with evil in the world by punishing it in His wrath on earth and in hell. In other words, Christians, churches and ministries have not given a solid reason to post-Christians for the hope that is in them (1 Pete 3:15). The reason we have not given a good, solid, compelling reason for our hope and faith is because we have eliminated the wrath of God and hell from the spiritual equation. Who needs your hope, your Christian faith or your God if there is no wrath of God or hell to punish all this evil our younger generations are seeing in our world. This is why Barna reported that 59% Gen Zers say *"church is not relevant to me personally"* (compared to 46% Christians and 64% non-Christians who say the same thing—that's right, 46% Christians are saying church is not relevant to them either for the same reason!); 27% Gen Zers say church involvement is *"not at all important"*; and only 20% Gen Zers say attending church is *"very important"*.

If Christians, churches and ministries would stop being weak phonies and just be real and shoot from the hip by telling people straight that God is dealing with all this evil in the world by punishing them in the fires of hell and with His wrath on earth in the End Times, you would see people in America embracing Christianity again and returning back to church again—in other words, you would see REVIVAL and a RE-AWAKENING in America again!

I'm not talking about beating people up with the teaching on God's wrath and hell in an angry or harsh way. I'm talking about giving people an equal amount of loving explanation, teaching and preaching about God's wrath and hell as you would about God's love and heaven. It's time we started giving God's wrath and hell equal time with God's love and heaven again in our witnessing, teaching and preaching. Gen Zers, Millennials and Gen Xers are looking for answers; not your half-truths about God being a good, loving God without explaining to them how God is also a severe God of wrath who punishes evil in this world and in hell.

This reality of God's wrath and hell needs to be shared unapologetically to Gen Zers, Millennials, Gen Xers, Baby Boomers and every other generation in America without trying to water it down because *there is no water* in hell. When Jesus was explaining the existence of hell to the crowds in Luke chapter 16:19–31, He told the people about an unnamed rich man and a poor man named Lazarus (not the same Lazarus that Jesus raised from the dead) who both died and were taken to Sheol (Hades). The rich man ended up in the hell side of Sheol (Hades) and the poor man ended up in the paradise side of Sheol (Hades). Jesus went on to tell the crowds that, *"In Hades* [the hell side of Hades], *where he* [the rich man] *was in torment, he* [the rich man] *looked up and saw Abraham far away* [on the paradise side of Hades], *with Lazarus by his side. So he* [the rich man] *called to him, 'Father Abraham, have pity on me and send Lazarus to dip the tip of his finger in water and cool my tongue, because I am in agony in this fire.'"* (Luke 16:22 NIV, bracketed emphasis mine) Jesus said hell is a place where people are in agony in fire with *no water* to cool them off. So why are you trying to water down God's wrath and hell? Just talk about God's wrath and hell the way Jesus talked about God's wrath and hell—that's *"what Jesus would do"*.

This decrease in church attendance in America started happening at the same time—30 years ago—when Christian churches and ministries in America started changing God's message to their own message by eliminating God's wrath and hell from their preaching and teaching. When are Christian churches and ministries in America going to wake up and realize that eliminating God's wrath and hell from their preaching and teaching isn't working for them or God's kingdom? By not talking about God's wrath and hell, the only thing these Christian churches and ministries are doing is sending people to hell. Think of the millions of souls in hell—Gen Zers, Millennials, Gen Xers, Baby Boomers and others—who are crying out to you Christians, churches and ministries saying, "*Why didn't you warn me about God's wrath and hell?! All you told me about was that God was a good, loving God; you never told me God is also severe!*"

Some of you, like so many post-Christians in America, are still having a hard time understanding how a loving God could send someone to hell. That's because you still don't realize God is not just a loving God; He's also a severe God. He is severe because He is holy and just; and a holy and just God must judge and punish sin and disobedience. Let God Himself describe Himself to you through the prophet Isaiah when God says, "*I, the LORD, will punish the world for its evil and the wicked for their sin. I will crush the arrogance of the proud and humble the pride of the mighty.*" (Isaiah 13:11 NLT)

There's no one to blame for this spiritual problem in America's younger generations of people except our present day Christian churches, ministers and ministries who have stopped educating people about God's wrath and hell. In their pursuit of the almighty dollar and larger attendances and audiences, which is nothing more than the fear and favor of man, these Christian churches, ministers and ministries have shot themselves in their own foot by removing the all-important components—God's wrath and hell—in their preaching and teaching that is the very thing that draws people back to Jesus Christ and the church. Christian churches and ministries have failed to do their part in giving the full counsel of God's word about the realities of heaven *and* hell, and about God's goodness *and* God's severity. It will be these Christian pastors, ministers, leaders, and the people in these Christian ministries and organizations that will have to give an account to Christ at the Judgment Seat of Christ on Judgment Day for failing to teach the full counsel of God about His wrath and the existence of hell, resulting in our nation's prodigal fall from God. That's why the Apostle James said, "*Not many of you should become teachers, my fellow believers, because you know that we who teach will be judged* [by Christ] *more strictly.*" (James 3:1 NIV, bracketed emphasis mine)

Right now, what's more important is getting these Christian churches, ministers and ministries to repent of their *sins of omission* (omitting God's wrath and hell) and start teaching and preaching the truth about God's wrath and hell again because **revival will never come back to America until Christians in America come back to preaching and teaching about God's wrath and hell**. Once these churches and Christian ministries repent of their *sins of omission* about God's wrath and hell, then our nation will once again see a revival of repentance among our people turning back to Christ and the church because our people will once again understand and appreciate their need to be rescued from the wrath of God and hell; they'll understand their need of a Savior.

Before our nation can experience revival and a re-awakening again, our Christian pastors, ministers, teachers, churches and ministries must be revived and re-awakened. Revival never happened in a city or nation without God first reviving and re-awakening a Christian who would stand up and speak out about God's word boldly and truthfully—that word of God includes speaking boldly about the reality of God's wrath and the existence of hell.

The Prodigal Son is a Homeless Person

We know that the prodigal son in Jesus' parable was homeless because Jesus said the prodigal son "*squandered his wealth in wild living. After he had spent everything, there was a severe famine in the whole country, and he began to be in need.*" (Luke 15:13–14 NIV) The prodigal son was broke, penniless and out on the streets. Most of us have seen a

120

homeless person begging on a street corner with a cardboard sign outstretched to passing cars filled with people looking the other way; carefully protecting their life's possessions jammed into a stolen shopping cart; lying hidden, almost unnoticed from the busy public's eye under the cover of cardboard, newspapers or a worn blanket; or resigned to sitting hopelessly on a sidewalk against a building or on a park bench as they stare aimlessly into a long lost, unreachable past.

What most of us have not seen is ourselves in that homeless person. That's because we don't realize we're looking at the man in the mirror. That homeless person you see on the street is a reflection of how we look in the spirit when we are habitually and constantly away from God's house and His people. We're "spiritually homeless" like that homeless person when we avoid going to church and being around God's people. That's how we look to God when we are separated from church trying to make it in life on our own without connecting with a body of believers.

There are many polling and statistical organizations, such as the Pew Research Center, Gallop, Barna and Statista that show a constant decline in church attendance in America over the years—less than 40 percent of Americans are attending religious services today. David Olson, the Director of Church Planting for the Evangelical Covenant Church, conducted extensive research that shows 17.7 percent (52 million) is a more realistic figure for "*actual regular church attendees*" in America today versus the 40 percent (132 million) "*church membership*" in America that pollsters like Gallop use to determine church attendance. Both percentages are bleak at best; and it continues to decline each year. In other words, the "*State of the Church in America*" is "homelessness"— Christians without a home; without a place they regularly go to worship God and fellowship with other Christians. Out on the streets instead of in the seats. Woody Allen said, "*Showing up is 80 percent of life.*" Clearly it is a no-show for Christianity when it comes to showing any life in churches in America. Christianity in America may have had a reputation of being alive in the past; but now it is on its last heartbeat. Jesus said it best this way: "*I know your deeds; you have a reputation of being alive, but you are dead.*" (Revelation 3:1 NIV)

Compare our church attendance numbers in America with other nations. At the top of the list of nations where Christians attend church at least once a week are African nations such as Nigeria (87%), Zambia (85%), Chad (83%), Ghana (82%), Uganda (81%) and Kenya (80%). Latin American nations also beat out the US in church attendance, such as Guatemala (78%), Honduras (70%), El Salvador (68%), Nicaragua (58%), Costa Rica (55%), Panama (51%), Brazil (49%) and Mexico (47%).

If Olsen's 17.7 percent is a more realistic figure for the actual number of Christians that regularly attend church in the America today, that means only 7 other nations have a lower church attendance rating than the US: Uruguay (16%), Germany (13%), Ukraine (13%), Lithuania (12%), Belgium (11%), France (11%) and Russia (8%) (Church Attendance–Wikipedia). We as Americans are on track to becoming the most godless nation on the planet—more godless than Russia at 8% church attendance.

Dr. J.D. Payne served as an Associate Professor of Church Planting and Evangelism in the Billy Graham School of Missions and Evangelism before becoming pastor of church multiplication at The Church at Brook Hills in Birmingham, Alabama. In Dr. Payne's report from the 2017 *Reaching the Nations Summit* that he posted at www.jdpayne.org, the United States now ranks as 3rd largest unreached people groups (282 people groups) in a nation among all the other countries in the world; with India being the 1st largest unreached nation (1,514 people groups) followed by China as the 2nd largest unreached nation (337 people groups) for Christ. An unreached people group is a group of people type in a nation that is less than 2% evangelical. These dismal statistics of Christianity in America also reveal that "*there is no evangelical church planting strategy being executed to reach that group*" in the US.

For those of you who think a calling from God to the mission field means a trip to Africa or some other foreign country, you had better rethink your mission focus—America is the new mission field . . . again. It's not Africa that's lacking in church attendance and the pursuit of God or is one of the largest unreached nations in the world; it's America! America is the nation that needs evangelizing more than Africa or many other foreign nations. That's how far Christianity in America has dropped over the years, and yet, Americans don't even realize this because we are spiritually asleep—we've been lulled to sleep by Satan. The Apostle Paul said, "*I am convinced that neither death nor life, neither angels nor demons, neither the present nor the future, nor any powers, neither height nor depth, nor anything else in all creation, will be able to separate us from the love of God that is in Christ Jesus our Lord.*" (Romans 8:38–39 NIV) The one thing Paul did not mention that could separate you from the love of God is you—just *you* asleep at the wheel when it comes to spiritual insight into America's true spiritual condition.

According to the Pew Research Center, in 1910, there were 66.3% of the world's Christians living in Europe compared to 4.5% Christians in Asia-Pacific, 1.4% in Sub-Saharan Africa, and 0.7% in Middle East-North Africa. Today, those figures are nearly reversed with only 25.9% of Christians now living in Europe compared to 23.6% Christians in Sub-Saharan Africa, 13.1% in Asia-Pacific, and 0.6% in Middle East-North Africa. The smaller number of Christians living in the Middle East-North Africa is attributed to the persecution of Christians that has been driving Christians out of those areas.

The data from the Pew Research Center shows that although Europe and the US still show a larger portion of Christians in the world, the number of Christians in Europe and the US have dropped drastically (95% in 1910 to 76.5% in 2010 for Europe; 96% in 1910 to 86% in 2010 for US), and the number of Christians in Africa and Asia-Pacific have increased (9% in 1910 to 63% in 2010 for Africa; 3% in 1910 to 7% in 2010 for Asia-Pacific). It won't be long before Christians in "Global South" countries (such as Africa, Latin America and Asia-Pacific countries) will outnumber Christians in "Global North" countries (such as North America, Europe, Australia, Japan and New Zealand).

Christianity in America has lost its spiritual sight and insight because American Christians do not realize that America is the country that needs evangelizing the most today; not Africa. It seems the only countries that are recognizing that America is now the new mission field are countries that America still thinks has the greatest need for evangelism—countries in Africa, Asia-Pacific and Latin America. That is why you are now starting to see more and more missionaries from other countries, such as Africa, Latin America and Asia-Pacific, coming to America to evangelize America!

What you are seeing happening today is something called "reverse missionaries" or "reverse evangelism" where missionaries and evangelists, such as Reinhard Bonnke, from former mission fields of "Global South" countries (such as Africa, Latin America and Asia-Pacific countries) are being called by God to evangelize people in "Global North" nations (such as European nations and the US) that are turning from God and becoming more secular. God now has to send evangelists and missionaries from nations in Africa, Latin America and Asia-Pacific to nations such as England and America to turn us back to God.

Take for instance Roselyn Inwe, the wife of Pastor Reuben Ekeme Inwe of the Nigerian Pentecostal megachurch Redeemed Christian Church of God (RCCG) in Lagos, Nigeria. Over 14 years ago, Roselyn also had a dream from God where she saw herself and her husband, Pastor Inwe, preaching before a white crowd of people, while what appeared as white sand to Roselyn that was falling on the building where they were preaching. They both interpreted her dream as God calling them to evangelize white British nonbelievers in the UK. Why? Because half of all British adults in the UK today have no religious affiliation, and church membership and attendance has declined drastically to half of what it was in the 1960s at all major Christian denominations in UK churches. Fast forward, God called Pastor Ekeme and Roselyn out of Nigeria, Africa to the UK in 2010 to start a new church in York, England called Hope Centre, York, a city of roughly 200,000 people of which 94% are white.

As Roselyn's dream became a reality as missionaries in the UK, they both realized that the white sand she saw in her dream was snow falling on the roof of their church building during the winter in England. The Inwe's home RCCG church in Nigeria, considered one of many diaspora churches around the world, now has over 800 branch churches in cities throughout England where they are reaching the white British population; and they have plans to plant hundreds more churches in the

UK while praying for spiritual revival in England. The RCCG church in Nigeria, as with many other churches from Africa and other Global South countries, are now sending missionaries and evangelists to America to turn our prodigal nation back to Christ.

America is no different than England and other nations, once thought of as a "city on a hill" and a "beacon of light" for Christianity, that are now becoming more secular, humanistic, materialistic and immoral. Christian churches in America now try to major in the "mega" and minor in the spiritual by avoiding teaching and preaching on hell and the wrath of God so as not to offend people. If Jesus were to describe Christianity in America, He would say, "*You have a name that you are alive, but you are dead.*" (Revelation 3:1 NKJV)

That's why Christianity in America needs revival just like the UK and other Global North countries once again. We need God to revive and awaken the spiritual in the hearts and minds of Americans. And in case you've been wondering, that's why America needs God to send missionaries and evangelists from other countries such as Africa, Latin America and Asia-Pacific countries to America and evangelize and revive us. Christianity in America is too spiritually blind and asleep to see it needs to evangelize and revive itself . . . again, the way we had done in past revivals such as the Great Awakening of England and the 13 colonies in America with Jonathan Edwards, John Wesley and George Whitefield between 1734 and 1743; the Second Great Awakening throughout America and England with James McGready and Charles Finney between 1800 and 1840; the Businessmen's Revival with Jeremiah Lanphier between 1857 and 1858; the Civil War Revival between 1861 and 1865; the Urban Revivals in Chicago with Dwight L. Moody between 1875 and 1885; the Revivals of 1905–1906 with Billy Sunday; the Azusa Street Revival in Los Angeles between 1906 and 1915 with William J. Seymour; and the Post-World War II Awakening and Revivals in America between 1910 and the 1970s with Billy Sunday, Bill Bright and Billy Graham.

What is revival? It's when God changes the cold, dead hearts of masses of people into living, passionate, burning hearts for Christ. It is many prodigal sons and daughters coming home all within the same timeframe in a church, in a city, in a nation. Revivals always emerge during times of spiritual and moral decay and decline of a city or nation, while God's people began to sincerely and intensely pray for the revival of its city and nation of hearts, minds and souls. That's why America is ripe for revival once again today—because America has declined spiritually and morally. That's why Christians in America must pray for revival and spiritual awakening once again; understanding full well that America is no longer that "city on a hill" but instead that "city in the swine pit" just as the prodigal son. The Bible tells us that *"the earnest (heartfelt, continued) prayer of a righteous man makes tremendous power available—dynamic in its working."* (James 5:16 AMP)

Africa, along with many other Global South countries, has learned to evangelize and revive themselves. That's why the population of Christians in Africa grew at an exponential rate from 10 million to 360 million in the 20th century alone; and at the amazing rate that Christianity in Africa is growing, it is expected that Christians in Africa will double in size by 2025, becoming perhaps the country with the largest Christian population in the world. Unfortunately, at the alarming rate at which Christianity in America is growing more as a secular prodigal nation that is running away from God, America will become a country with one of the smallest Christian populations in the world.

That's why attendance in Christian churches in America has dropped so drastically as in England. We Christians who are "missing in action" from church are no different than a homeless person who has gone missing on the streets when we're away from God's house and His people. We're no different than a homeless person who is isolated, separated and removed from family, friends and society when we isolate, separate and remove ourselves from the society of family and friends within God's house—the church. We don't realize that we're *"poor in spirit"* like the homeless poor begging on a street corner when we remove ourselves from our brothers and sisters in Christ who are well-fed in God's house. Like a homeless person who blindly wanders from place to place, we blindly wander away from connecting with God's people in church. Like so many poorly clothed homeless people you've seen on the streets, we refuse to be clothed with the fellowship of God's people. Just as so many homeless on the city streets of our neighborhood have thrown away so many opportunities, gifts, friendships, resources and help offered them in life, we throw away the opportunities, gifts, friendships, resources and help God is trying to give us in and through the people He is trying to connect us with in our local church and a body of believers. We're continuously falling over the cliff and spiraling further downward toward our death at the dark bottom—just as in my recurring nightmares.

The problem for prodigal America is we don't see ourselves as homeless—spiritually homeless that is. Most of us see ourselves as having a place of residence that gives us the illusion that we're secure under the safety of a roof over our heads. Since we're not physically out on the street, living out of a car, covered under a cardboard box, huddled under a makeshift tent or sleeping under a bridge; we count ourselves among those who are well-off and fortunate enough to have money, a roof over our head and food on our table. We can afford a house, an apartment or some other accommodation. We content ourselves with the fact that we have a job with benefits, a business, a retirement pension, an inheritance, royalties, investments, stocks and bonds or other sources of income— *"We have what we need, why do we need church?"* To spiritually homeless people who feel content and satisfied to remain away from church, Jesus has this to say: *"You claim to be rich and successful and to have everything you need. But you don't know how bad off you really are. You are pitiful, poor, blind and naked."* (Revelation 3:17 CEV) It's time for us to take a good look at ourselves in the mirror of God's word.

Many people attend church "their way" instead of "God's way", just as Cain gave an offering to God his way instead of God's way. We substitute watching Christian programming on TV or online or reading the Bible at home or giving to charities online in place of actually attending church. Like Cain who gave God the substitutes of disobedience, we think these substitutes for attending church will please God. However, our substitutes do not satisfy God when it comes to church attendance any more than Cain's substitute for worshipping God because we're doing it our own way instead of God's way.

Don't go it alone. Don't try to do this Christian life alone and away from God's house and His people. You weren't created by God to go it alone. You were created by God to do this Christian life together with other Christians. The formula for success and happiness in the Christian life is to do it with God's house and His people; not doing it alone by ourselves away from God's house and His people. We belong in God's house with His people. That's our natural and normal place of residence as Christians. That's where we belong. God designed it that way. God designed us to live, grow and develop in His house among His people.

The Bible says, *"Some people have given up the habit of meeting for worship, but we must not do that. We should keep on encouraging each other, especially since you know that the day of the Lord's coming is getting closer."* (Hebrews 10:25 CEV) This seemingly simple little act of disobedience of not attending church may seem harmless to us but it is the kind of prideful disobedience that can cause God's opposition, resistance and lack of peace in different areas of our life—just like with Cain. God does not want your substitute for attending church; God wants *you* attending church. Will we choose to obey or disobey God's will and desire for us to return to His house and His people?

The Prodigal Son is a Deceived and Misguided Person

Prodigal people do not realize that the church *is* the body of Christ. In other words, you cannot separate Christ's body—the church—and Christ. If we separate and isolate ourselves from the church, we are separating and isolating ourselves from Christ. This is one of the greatest deceptions that Satan uses to mislead so many Christians into separating themselves from Jesus. Satan has deceived so many Christians into thinking we can separate the church from Christ the way our government has tried to separate church and state. When we say we can seek Christ alone without having to go to church; we are effectively saying we can hang out with Jesus but not Jesus' body—it can't be done. That's Satan's deception that prodigal children have fallen for. That was the deception that I fell for many times in my Christian life. In a prodigal person's deceived mindset, it *can* be done; therefore, we act it out in our lives as if it were possible. Prodigal children think, talk and walk as if we are wise, but such thoughts, words and actions only makes us fools. *"Professing to be wise, they became fools . . . who exchanged the truth of God for the lie."* (Romans 1:22, 25 NKJV)

It's kind of like the Hans Christian Andersen tale of *The Emperor's New Clothes*. In this tale, the emperor believed the lies of swindlers that told him he was wearing special, beautiful clothing that only people who were stupid or unworthy could not see. Even though the emperor himself could not see the clothing (because there was none), he did not want others to think he was stupid or unworthy; therefore, he walked around in public with no clothes on thinking he was fully clothed. Even when a child proclaimed, *"The emperor hasn't got anything on!"* the emperor was too proud to admit he wasn't wearing any clothes and continued thinking, talking and walking foolishly through the streets with no clothes on.

Just as the emperor in this story who spoke and acted as if he were wise, Satan has swindled Christians into thinking we are wise and fully clothed when in fact we're foolishly naked in the spirit when we're away from church. Satan has sold Christians a false bill of goods. He has swindled and convinced Christians into thinking we are completely clothed with a relationship with Christ when in fact our spirit is unclothed because we avoid the *body* of Christ—the church.

Sure, we read our Bible, pray and worship God but we do it in our own way alone and away from church and God's people. After all, *"we don't need them"*, we tell ourselves. *"We can have a relationship with God without having a relationship without His people. We can read the Bible on our own at home without having to go to church to hear the Bible read to us. We can pray by ourselves without having to pray with people in church. Besides, didn't the Bible say something about us going into our closets of privacy and pray? I can listen or watch my favorite minister on TV or online. I can worship in the privacy of my own home without having to worship together with other people at church. I don't need to go to church to live out my Christian life. God sees my heart."*

Do you want to know what Jesus sees when He looks at our heart with those thoughts, attitude and behavior toward His bride which is those believers at church? Jesus said, *"I know your works, that you are neither cold nor hot. I could wish you were cold or hot. So then, because you are lukewarm, and neither cold nor hot, I will vomit you out of My mouth. Because you say, 'I am rich, have become wealthy, and have need of nothing'—and do not know that you are wretched, miserable, poor, blind, and naked."* (Revelation 3:15–17 NKJV)

It's true that even Christ took time away from His disciples and the crowds and withdrew often to a lonely place to pray. (Luke 5:16) However, Jesus did not stay there. He came out of His prayer closet to be with God's people too. If God has given us the power to leave our home, we have the power to go to church. Do you have the power to go to the grocery store to buy a loaf of bread? If the answer is a resounding yes, then you have the power to go to church to be fed the bread of life. Are you physically able to drive your car where you need to be? Then you are physically able to drive yourself to church where you need to be. Are you going to the gym to work out your body? Then you have to power to go to church and work out your spiritual muscles. Do you enjoy going out to a restaurant, theater, concert, sports game or other activities outside your home? Then you have the power to enjoy going out to a church activity. If you have time, money and energy to go shopping or take a trip or vacation; then you have time, money and energy available to take a trip to your local church. If you have the ability to walk out the door of your residence to work in a job or go to school or visit a friend or family member; then you have the ability to visit and attend a local church in your area. If God has given you the strength to do any of these things outside of church, He has given you the strength to physically do things with His people in church.

Watching Christians worshiping in church from a distance by watching them online or on TV or listening on the radio is not the same as being there in person. It's not enough to read our Bible alone, pray alone or worship God alone. God meant for us to be together hearing His word together, praying together and worshiping the Lord together. If you're watching God from a distance by watching and listening to Christian ministers and programs on TV, online and on the radio, don't stop. That's a good thing you're doing, but don't stop there. You were meant for more as a Christian. God intended you to have more and experience more in the family of God.

Did you grow up with family members—a father, mother, grandparents, foster parents, brothers, sisters, aunts, uncles, nieces or nephews? Now imagine what it would be like if you never saw those family members throughout your life growing up. Imagine a life where you only communicated with your family members on Skype, Facebook, FaceTime, Snapchat, Twitter or some other social media site; and never ever saw them in person. Is it the same thing as them being there in person? Do you really think you would have experienced the things you have in life by that kind of "distant relationship"? Do you think you would have learned the things you learned in life; laughed the way you laughed in life; cried the tears you cried in life; or grown the way you grew up in life without your family members physically being there with you? Of course not. Why? Because nothing beats having your family members there in person. It's no different when watching or listening to Christian programming from a distance on TV, radio or online—you can't experience the same Christian life God wants you to experience from a distance. You have to be there in person with God's people. You can't develop fully and properly as a Christian the way God wants you to develop without physical interaction with other Christians in church.

Watching and listening to those Christian activities happening on TV, online and radio is only a *supplement*; it is not a *substitute* for us physically being in those activities ourselves. Nothing can substitute or replace you being with the body of Christ; not TV, not online, not radio, not anything. Watching and listening to Christian programming on TV, online and radio was meant to only supplement the real thing; it was never meant to replace the real thing, just like social media was never meant to replace your real family and friends. The real thing is actually being in God's house with God's people, hearing God's word with God's people, worshiping God with His people, serving our community with His people and getting to know God more with His people.

Perhaps you've watched a program showing how a pack of predator animals, such as lions or wolves, will try to isolate one of their preys from the rest of the herd in order to take down that single lone prey. That's what Satan and his pack of demons are trying to do to us as Christians. Their strategy and goal is to separate and isolate you from the rest of the Christian herd by getting you to stop attending church in order to control and manipulate you more so they can take you down and render you unfruitful and ineffective for God's kingdom purposes. That's why the Bible tells us to *"be alert and of sober mind. Your enemy the devil prowls around like a roaring lion looking for someone to devour"*. (1 Peter 5:8 NIV)

Jesus said, *"The thief* [Satan] *comes only to steal and kill and destroy."* (John 10:10 NIV, bracketed emphasis mine) In Matthew chapter 13, Jesus tells the parable of the sower to explain the strategy Satan, the thief, uses to steal, kill and destroy our relationship with God and separate us from Jesus. As Jesus shares this parable of a farmer who went out to sow his seed, He talked about the seeds that fell along the path that the birds came and ate up; seeds that fell on rocky, shallow soil that produced plants that withered because of a shallow root base; seeds that fell among thorns that choked the plants as they grew; and seeds that fell on good soil that produced a fruitful crop.

The seed sown along the path instead of deep fertile soil is when Satan snatches or steals God's word from people's hearts because they did not understand the reflection of the man in the mirror of Gods' word shown to their heart. These people don't get all the fuss about attending church. They don't understand the connection between Christ's body—the church—and Christ Himself. The Bible says, *"Just as the body is one and has many members, and all the members of the body, though many, are one body, so it is with Christ."* (1 Corinthians 12:12 ESV) Have you understood that Jesus and His body—the church—are one and the same in God's eyes, or has Satan snatched this truth from your heart?

The seed sown on shallow, rocky soil are people who have a shallow heart that doesn't allow God's word to take deep root in their heart. As a result, when something offends, disappoints or bothers them, they're the first to complain, give up, throw in the towel and leave the church. They were there only temporarily in God's house with His people singing and rejoicing and serving; but then you don't see them anymore. Where are they? They're home licking their wounds, separated and isolated from church, just the way "the thief" planned it. The predator (Satan) has separated them from the herd (church).

When the prophet Elijah ran away and separated and isolated himself in a cave, God said to him, *"What are you doing here, Elijah?"* (1 Kings 19:9) If you've decided to "home-church" yourself the way some people homeschool their children, God is saying to you: *"What are you doing here?"* Now more than ever in these "Last Days", we need to be with God's people when the predator of our souls tries to discourage us from attending church. Greg Laurie, the senior pastor of Harvest Christian Fellowship in Riverside, California, Harvest Church at Kumulani in Kapalua, Hawaii, and Harvest Orange County in Irvine, California said, *"When we are depressed, it is not the time to isolate ourselves from God's people."*

The seeds that fell among thorns that choked the plants as they grew are people who allow the worries and cares of this world and the deceitfulness of wealth, fame, success and possessions to crowd out, choke and lure them away from God's word and a healthy, fruitful relationship with God and His people. I get it, there's a lot in this world to care and worry about, but we shouldn't allow the latest news be the headline of our hearts. The Good News of God's word and His kingdom should be on the front page of our hearts. Jesus Himself said, *"You will hear of wars and rumors of wars, but see to it that you are not alarmed. Such things must happen, but the end is still to come. Nation will rise against nation, and kingdom against kingdom. There will be famines* and earthquakes in various places. All these are the beginning of birth pains." (Matthew 24:6–8 NIV)

Notice also that Jesus did not say *wealth* or *riches* choke God's word out of your heart and life because wealth and riches in and of itself is not bad or evil. There's nothing wrong with having wealth, riches and prosperity. Jesus said the "*deceitfulness of wealth*" chokes Gods word out of your heart and life. (Matthew 13:22) The Bible didn't say "money" is the root of all kinds of evil. The Bible says the "*love of money" is the root of all kinds of evil.* (1 Timothy 6:10) Wealth, riches and prosperity is one of the most powerful tools in supporting God's kingdom purposes. Some of the most generous and philanthropic people in the world are wealthy people. Where would ministries be today without the tithes and offerings that come from the blessings of wealth, riches and prosperity of our country's citizens. You can't give to ministries and people in need if you don't have any money to give. You must be blessed in order to be a blessing to others. You must have money to give money to people and to support Christian causes.

There's nothing wrong or evil with you having money; the problem is when money has a hold of you. If wealth was evil, God would not have made people like Abraham, Isaac, Jacob, David and Solomon rich. Concerning king Solomon's wealth, God said to him, "*Since this is your heart's desire* [wisdom] *and you have not asked wealth, possession or honor, nor for the death of your enemies, and since you have not asked for a long life but for wisdom and knowledge to govern my people over whom I have made you king, therefore wisdom and knowledge will be given you. And I will also give you wealth, possessions and honor, such as no king who was before you ever had and none after you will have.*" (2 Chronicles 1:11–12 NIV, bracketed emphasis mine) In today's currency, it is estimated that Solomon was worth over $64,300,800,000 dollars. That's over $64.3 billion with a "b" baby!

To say wealth is evil is to say God is evil who created wealth and made these men rich. To say wealth is evil is to say God is evil because God is wealthy. God said, "*Every animal in the forest belongs to Me, and so do the cattle on a thousand hills. I know all the birds in the mountains, and every wild creature is in my care. If I were hungry, I wouldn't tell you, because I own the world and everything in it."* (Psalm 50:10–12 CEV) If wealth is evil, God would not have paved His streets in heaven with gold; built the walls of the heavenly Jerusalem city with precious stones; or crowned His 24 elders around His thrown with golden crowns. If wealth is evil, the streets of heaven would be dirt paths; the heavenly city would be walled off with stacks of cardboard; and everyone in heaven would be wearing paper party hats. No, the possession of wealth is merely a sign of prosperity; not a sign of evil. It's when wealth possesses you that it becomes a sign of evil.

The majority of people who flocked to the California God Rush in the 1840s to the 1850s left broke and empty-handed; however, that gold fever produced the largest mass migration in our nation's history with roughly 300,000 people that came to California from other parts of the US and abroad. The odds of winning the Powerball lottery are 1 in 292.2 million—has this stopped you from buying tickets? Addictions.com showed 80 percent of American adults gamble on a yearly basis and up to 750,000 young people, ages 14 to 21 have a gambling addiction— legalized online sports betting will increase those numbers. All of these are signs of wealth possessing people; not people possessing wealth.

People have become such hoarders of "stuff"; it has become a serious disorder in many countries including the US. Just look at how much stuff we have stored in our homes, closets, garages and storage units. We're a nation of stuff, too much stuff. We have so much stuff that it oftentimes leaves little room in our precious space for God's word in our hearts. We're a nation that prides itself in the stuff we have, the stuff we do and the stuff we experience in places we've been. We only have to look at our social media posts to know this is true of ourselves. We get drawn in by the roses only to get pricked and caught in the thorns, just like the seeds sown among thorns. If you are struggling with a problem with materialism or hoarding stuff, I recommend reading the book *Money, Possessions, and Eternity* by Randy Alcorn.

The seeds that fell on good soil that produced a fruitful crop are people who hear God's word, understand it and produce fruit. They have a healthy relationship with Jesus and His body—the church. They have not allowed Satan to separate them from Jesus. They are where they're supposed to be—with God and His people; doing what they're supposed to be doing—fellowshipping, worshipping and serving together as one body in Christ. Notice that it is this healthy relationship with God and His people—the church—that is the seed sown on the good soil of one's heart that Satan cannot steal, kill or destroy. That's because your blessing, anointing and protection is increased when you are with God's people.

When the seed of God's word hits our heart, is it falling on something as hard as a cement pathway; is it buried just beneath the surface of shallow ground; is it caught immediately in the death grip of distracting thorns; or will those seeds take deep root in good soil that will produce abundant fruit in our life? What strategy has Satan used in our life to try to deceive and misguide us into being separated and isolated from Jesus and church?

The Prodigal Son Always Has an Excuse

Part of the reason God gave me those recurring dream nightmares for 7 nights in a row of looking over my shoulder at that house—that I now know was a church—that I was running away from before falling over that cliff was God wanted to warn me about what would happen in my future so that I could learn to change the outcome and return back to God's house and His people. Having lived out that dream as a recurring prodigal son a good portion of my Christian life, I got real good at making excuses for not going to church. There was no end to the excuses Satan would feed me to sift me like wheat in order to keep me separated from Jesus by keeping me separated from His body—the church. If there's an excuse you've probably used for not going to church, I've probably already used it. What's your excuse for not going to church?

Was it someone who offended you at church? Get over it and find another church where you feel more welcomed. Better yet, learn to forgive your brother or sister the way Christ forgave you, and reconcile your differences with them. (Ephesians 4:32) The Apostle Paul tells us, *"Make allowance for each other's faults, and forgive anyone who offends you. Remember, the Lord forgave you, so you must forgive others."* (Colossians 3:13 NLT)

Was it "all those hypocrites" in the church you couldn't stand? I heard someone once say that if God removed all the hypocrites out of church and put you in that church, there'd be another hypocrite in the church again—you. Adlai E. Stevenson said, *"A hypocrite is the kind of politician who would cut down a redwood tree, then mount the stump and make a speech for conservation."* As you mount your stump and make your speech about all those hypocrites in church, have you ever stopped to wonder if you've ever said one thing and done another? Jesus put it this way: *"Let him who is without sin among you be the first to cast a stone."* (John 8:7 ESV) What's the cure for this excuse for not being in church? Try removing the log from that redwood tree stump. Jesus said, *"First get rid of the log from your own eye; then perhaps you will see well enough to deal with the speck in your friend's eye."* (Matthew 7:5 NLT)

Are you fearful of what they might think of you in church? Then take a family member or friend with you to give you the courage to check out churches in your local area.

True story, after a long absence of several years being away from church, God finally convinced me to return to church—that house in my recurring dream. The problem was I was too afraid to walk through the doors of a church again. The devil had me so spooked about what to say in church, what to do, how to act, what they would think, what they would do, how they would act—all those stupid things the devil will put in my head just to prevent me from walking through the doors of a church.

Satan and his pack of demons used these thoughts to successfully separate me from God's herd.

Although I still didn't think I could go through with it, I decided I was going to at least get dressed for church one Sunday morning and drive myself to a local church I had researched online earlier and thought would be worth checking out. So I drove alone to that church, pulled into the parking lot, and just sat there in my car trying to convince myself to open the door of my car and step out. I decided I couldn't go through with it and drove home.

Not to be outdone by the enemy that easily, the next Sunday, I got dressed for church again, got in my car and drove to that same church. Again, I only got as far as that church's parking lot; freaked out with fear, and decided to turn around and go home instead of going into that church.

Guess what I did the third Sunday? You guessed it. I got dressed for church again, got in my car and drove to that same church again. This time I got enough courage to get out of my car and walk through the doors of that church, knees knocking and all. And you know what I discovered? All those people I was afraid of were the nicest people I ever met. I realized then that all the fear I was experiencing was just the lies of the devil keeping me away from God's house and His people. I ended up joining that church, and later became an usher in that church so that I could welcome other people who walked through that church door.

All along, our loving Father God was waiting for me to come home to church in order to love me and bless me the same way that father was waiting for his prodigal son to return home so he could shower him with his love. God wasn't waiting at the door to scold or punish me. He was waiting for me to return so He could forgive me and restore to me all the things I missed out on being away from His house and His people. In the parable of the prodigal son that returned home, Jesus said, "*The father said to his servants, 'Bring out the best robe and put it on him* [the prodigal son], *and put a ring on his hand and sandals on his feet. And bring the fatted calf here and kill it, and let us eat and be merry; for this my son was dead and is alive again; he was lost and is found.' And they began to be merry.*" (Luke 15:22–24 NKJV, bracketed emphasis mine)

Why go through what I went through—bring a family member, a friend, your neighbor's kid, a dog, your pet turtle, or a squirrel from your backyard; bring whatever you need along with you for some moral support if that's what it takes to get you to check out a local church in your area. You'll save yourself some money for gas in the process too.

Do you simply not like "church people"? Do they get on your nerves with their "*halleluiahs*" and "*praise the Lord*"? This may come as a shocker to you but God did not say you had to *like* them; He said you have to *love* them because it's love that covers a multitude of sins. (1 Peter 4:8) Jesus commanded us to love one another (John 13:34) but He never commanded us to like one another. It's no different with your enemies. When Jesus said, "*Love your enemies*" (Matthew 5:44), He didn't say you had to like your enemies. He just said, "*Love your enemies*" because it is love that covers a multitude of your enemies' sins.

What you need to realize is that God did not *like* you in your fallen state of sin because you were His enemy—that's why He was not going to allow you into His kingdom the way you were. But He *loved* you enough to send His own Son to die on the cross in your place for your sins to make you righteous and holy in His sight so that He could allow you into His kingdom. That, my friend, took God loving you when He didn't like you. God does not love you because Christ died for you; Christ died for you because God loves you. The Bible explains God's love for you this way: "*God demonstrates His own love for us, in that while we were still sinners* [someone He didn't like], *Christ died for us.*" (Romans 5:8 NET, bracketed emphasis mine) Did you get that? While you were a person He didn't like, Christ died for you because you were a person He *loved*.

Jesus wasn't just giving you a command when He said, "*A new command I give you: Love one another. As I have loved you, so you must love one another.*" (John 13:34 NIV) What Jesus was giving you was a lesson on how to love someone you don't like. And who better to teach you this lesson than the One who died for you while you were someone He didn't like—a sinner. I know you think you're all that and a bag of chips; but what you need to understand like all the rest of us is that Christ died for you because He loved you; not because He liked you. This is not your *As the World Turns* soap opera love. This is God's *out of this world* kind of love. This is why you need Christ's love in you to help you love someone you don't like, the way Christ loved you. (Galatians 2:20) And now that Jesus has cleansed you from your sins, He not only loves you, He *likes you* too.

The Apostle John said, *"Whoever does not love their brother and sister, whom they have seen, cannot love God, whom they have not seen."* (1 John 4:20 NIV) There are people in church I love that I don't necessarily like. Don't look at me that way. You probably have some kids of your own that you love that you don't necessarily like, especially as they get older. I don't recommend you telling your kids that; but it's crossed your mind a time or two. Perhaps it's another family member or relative that gets on your nerves. You don't like them but somehow you've found a way to love them despite the fact that they are getting on your last nerve. Some of you so-called "spiritual ones" are still looking at me like you don't know what I'm talking about; so let me help you adjust your halo a little bit.

Let's be real for just one Jesus minute here. No matter what spiritual metaphor or words you try to couch your response in or no matter how many pretty little religious bows and ribbons you try to wrap around your answer, the fact remains that there are some people in this world you simply do not like although you know God commands you to love them. Do any of you have kids that are grown and gone or relatives that don't live with you? Now how many of you have no problem whatsoever with those grown kids or your in-laws or that crazy uncle coming to live with you permanently? Can I get a crazy *"Amen"*? I'm hearing a resounding *"Not no, but* [fill in the blank] *no!"* from you now. Why? Because you love them ('cause we family) but you don't like them enough to have them live with you permanently day in and day out.

That's how it is with people in church too. We don't mind "fellowshipping" with them at church but there is no way in God's green planet we want to live with some of them. Why? Because we love all of them as the family of God but we don't like all of them enough to have them live with us day in and day out. There are many people in church of a different political party than me or which I have absolutely nothing in common with except the fact that we both love Jesus; but that's all it takes—Christ in us—for us to love one another despite our differences.

Some of you are being set free with this revelation right now from the false condemnation of the devil that has been making you feel guilty for not liking some of the people in your church. It's ok to not like them; God probably doesn't like them either but He still loves them just like He loves you (I didn't say God doesn't like you).

We know that we have passed from death to life, because we love other believers. The person who doesn't grow in love remains in death. (John 3:14 GWT)

The one who loves his brother abides in the Light and there is no cause for stumbling in him. (1 John 2:10 NASB)

Everyone who hates his fellow Christian is a murderer, and you know that no murderer has eternal life residing in him. (1 John 3:15 NET Bible)

Although God wants you to *love*—though He knows you may not *like*—all your brothers and sisters in Christ, He never wants you to hate them. Hatred is what caused Cain to attack and kill his brother Abel. (Genesis 4:8) When you hate your brother or sister in Christ, the Lord sees you as hating Him. When you hold a grudge against a believer, Jesus sees you holding that grudge against Him. When you slander or judge another Christian, Jesus sees you slandering and judging Him. When you choose to avoid Christians by not going to church, Jesus sees you avoiding Him.

Remember when Saul, before his conversion to Paul the Apostle, was breathing out murderous threats against Christians? While traveling on the road to Damascus to imprison and persecute more Christians, the Lord Jesus knocked Saul off his high horse of self-righteousness and said to him, "*Saul, Saul, why do you persecute Me?*" (Acts 9:1–4 NIV) Not "*Why do you persecute these believers*" but "*Why do you persecute **Me**".* Jesus viewed Saul's attacks against Christians as a personal affront against Himself. That's because Jesus sees Himself and His bride—the church—as one and the same. If someone was attacking your spouse, wouldn't you see that as an attack against you? (If you are having issues with your spouse, don't answer that.) Jesus said, "*Truly I tell you, whatever you did for one of the least of these brothers and sisters of mine, you did for me . . . whatever you did not do for one of the least of these, you did not do for me.*" (Matthew 25:40, 46 NIV)

Do you need more evidence that God exists and that heaven and hell is for real before you seek God and return to church? Trust me, if you don't accept the evidence of the Bible that God is giving you right now, you'll have all the evidence you need in the hell the Bible is warning you about. Don't take my word for it; just listen to the word of God spoken by Jesus in the Bible. In Luke 16:19–31 that I shared earlier, Jesus was explaining the existence of God and the reality of paradise and hell to the crowds when He told them the true story of a rich man and a poor man Lazarus who both died and were taken to Sheol (Hades). As I mentioned earlier, the rich man ended up in the hell side of Sheol (Hades) and the poor man ended up with Abraham in the paradise side of Sheol. The rich man who was in torment in hell begged Abraham to send Lazarus back from the place of the dead to warn his five living brothers about the reality of hell. In response, Abraham replied, "*They have Moses and the Prophets* [in other words, they have the word of God]; *let them listen to them.*" (Luke 16:29 NIV, bracketed emphasis mine) The rich man knew his five brothers would ask for more evidence before believing and turning to God; therefore, "*The rich man replied, 'No, Father Abraham! But if someone is sent to them from the dead, then they will repent of their sins and turn to God.*'" (Luke 16:30 NLT)

What Abraham told that rich man is what I'm telling those of you who say you need more evidence that God exists and that heaven and hell is for real before you seek God and return to church: Abraham said to him, *"If they do not listen to Moses and the Prophets* [in the word of God], *they will not be convinced even if someone rises from the dead* [to tell them about the realities of hell]." (Luke 16:31 NIV, bracketed emphasis mine)

Are you simply too busy to attend church? A church service lasts roughly one hour. In your busy life of 168 hours a week, not enough time, huh? How about your busy life of 336 hours every two weeks—schedule still too full with work, school, sleep, golf, hours upon hours of television, eating in, eating out and hanging out, exercise, staring at your phone, walking the dog and recreation to find time for one hour of church attendance every two weeks? Perhaps you could fit in one hour of church attendance in the 672 hours every person has each month—you can't because you're waiting on that all-important phone call from the *Justice League?* Got it.

Listen, we can play this game all day but the fact is we need to stop making excuses for not going to church and start finding reasons to start attending church. The type of heart we have, the type of life we live and the type of fruit we bear in life depends on it. King Solomon said, *"Guard your heart above all else, for it determines the course of your life."* (Proverbs 4:23 NLT)

Every species of animal, fish and bird knows by nature how to return home to where they belong—whether it is mule deer or elk migrating to better feeding ground, salmon swimming upstream to spawn or swallows flying south for the winter. It's only mankind who has trouble finding his way back home to God's house—just like me in my recurring dreams.

God has given us the right to be in His house with His people because Jesus died on the cross for our sins—period, end of story. Jesus wants us to be with Him *and* His people, both here on earth and in heaven. We're a part of the family of God. If we're having trouble being around Christians in church here on earth, we're really going to have a problem being around each other in eternity. You have a free ticket to the house of God. In fact, He's given you the keys to the place. Jesus said, "*I will give you the keys of the kingdom of heaven.*" (Matthew 16:19 NIV) It's not just His house; it's your house as a child of God. Jesus paid for your place at the table in His house by His blood on that cross at Calvary. Your loving Father God is waiting for you to come home, just like the prodigal son's father was waiting for his son to return home. Like the prodigal son's father, your loving heavenly Father God is longing to embrace you in His arms and shower you with His love when you return home to church.

God's invitation for you to come home is still open. God is saying to you, "*Come, let us discuss this, says the LORD. Though your sins are like scarlet, they will be as white as snow, though they are as red as crimson, they will be like wool. If you are willing and obedient, you will eat the good of the land. But if you refuse and rebel, you will be devoured by the sword. For the mouth of the LORD has spoken*". (Isaiah 1:18–20 HCSB)

I realize all churches are not created equal. It may take you some time to do some research online like I did, asking your friends or cruising around your neighborhood to find a local church that looks worth checking out. Take all the time you need, but by all means, take the time to look for a local church in your area to attend. Don't allow Satan to feed you one excuse after another for burying your gifts and talents in the privacy of your own home because of a lame excuse, unforgiveness or bitterness about a past offense or fear of walking through the doors of a church. Don't be that servant who said to his master, "*I was afraid, and I went and hid your talent in the ground.*" (Matthew 25:25 ESV) If we say that, Jesus will say to us what that master said to his servant: "*You wicked, lazy servant!*" (Matthew 25:26 NIV) Learn to share yourself, your gifts and your talents for God's purposes and kingdom with God's people; and you will hear your Master Jesus say to you, "*Well done, good and faithful servant!*" (Matthew 25:21, 23 NIV)

The Prodigal Son's Return Home

It's amazing how great God's loving heart of grace and compassion truly is. He is willing and able to rescue the worst of us—if we would just humble ourselves before Him. I can't tell you how many times I became the prodigal son and left God and church because it's been more times than I can remember. But each time I was ready to come home, God was there waiting for me with open, loving arms. The Bible tells us, *"He [God], being full of compassion, forgave their iniquity, and did not destroy them. Yes, many a time He turned His anger away, and did not stir up all His wrath; for He remembered that they were but flesh, a breath that passes away and does not come again."* (Psalm 78:38–39 NKJV, bracketed emphasis mine)

Of all the wicked kings of Israel and Judah of whom the Bible repeatedly stated *"did evil in the eyes of the Lord"*, no king was considered more evil than wicked Ahab, king of Israel. In 1 Kings 21:25 (ISV), the Bible tells us, *"It can be truly said that no one else sold himself to practice what the LORD considered to be evil quite like the way Ahab did, because his wife Jezebel incited him."* Because Ahab constantly disobeyed the Lord, God pronounced His death sentence upon Ahab through the prophet Elijah (1 kings 21:17–19, 21–25). But when Ahab heard from Elijah how God would resist and oppose him to the point of death for his pride and sin, he tore his clothes and lay in sackcloth, and went about mourning under the weight of God's judgment pronounced upon his life. In other words, wicked Ahab humbled himself before God. Did you hear what I just said? Ahab, one of the most wicked persons recorded in the Bible, humbled himself before God. And how did God respond to Ahab's humility?

God responded by saying to the prophet Elijah, *"See how Ahab has humbled himself before Me? Because he has humbled himself before Me, I will not bring the calamity in his days."* (1 Kings 21:29 NKJV) WOW! God just did a complete 180 on the most wicked person in His sight—someone God *hated*—at that time in Bible history. What amazing grace! What an amazing tender heart God's heart is that can be moved to such a degree of compassion on the most wicked person recorded in the Bible when that person humbled himself before God! That means there's hope for you and me when we humble ourselves and return home to God and church. "*So humble yourselves under the mighty power of God, and at the right time He will lift you up in honor.*" (1 Peter 5:6 NLT)

When God had enough with the kings of Judah because of their disobedience, He sent prophets to tell the nation of Judah about their impending doom and captivity in Babylon in the same way the nation of Israel was taken captive to Assyria. When Josiah, king of Judah at that time, heard the words of God's judgment upon his nation of Judah, he too humbled himself before the Lord as king Ahab had done. (2 Kings 22:11–20) What was God's response to Josiah?

God's heart of compassion said to Josiah, "*Because your heart was tender, and you humbled yourself before the LORD . . . and you tore your clothes and wept before Me, I also have heard you . . . you shall be gathered to your grave in peace; and your eyes shall not see all the calamity which I will bring on this place.*" (2 Kings 22:19–20 NKJV)

So what does it take to return home to God or His people—the church? Do we need to clean up our act and stop sinning before coming back to God or church? No. Do we need to start reading our Bible first or perform some random acts of kindness first before visiting our local church? No. Then what must we do before returning to God or church? Nothing. All God wants you to do is simply come as you are, warts and all. Just take that first step of returning to God and church, and God will do the rest for you. He will change you from the inside out. He will turn things around and get your life moving in the right direction. Trust Him and move forward in the direction of His house the way I and that prodigal son in Jesus' story took our first step to return home; and your heavenly Father will do the rest.

In the incredible true story retold in the book *The Girl With No Name*, a little 4-year-old girl was abducted; dragged deep into the jungle from her remote mountain village in South America; and left there to die in her painful terror and loneliness, constant cries for help and never-ending tears. Though her tears and cries for help would go unanswered by any human ear, the Lord Jesus saw her tears and answered her cries for help. After several days and nights wandering aimlessly and fearfully into this wild jungle filled with dangerous animals, the Lord led this little helpless, hungry, thirsty, dying child to fresh water to quench her thirst and a family of monkeys who rescued and raised her in the jungle.

After the curious monkeys cautiously approached her, poked and pulled at this frightened little girl, over time they accepted her into their clan; began showing her berries and other jungle food she could eat; groomed her by picking the bugs and lice out of her hair like they did for the other monkeys; taught her how to survive in the jungle; and protected her like one of their own. It was like something out of a *Tarzan* or *The Jungle Book* movie. She began following them; doing what they were doing; eating what they were eating; surviving for years in the jungle with these monkeys without any human contact. After years of living among these monkeys in the jungle, her memory of her past human life was gone. She learned to climb and live and play in the trees with her monkey family. She would only make grunting sounds like the monkeys and no longer uttered any words of her native language; and her actions mimicked more of her foster family of monkeys than human behavior.

One day a few years later, the Lord allowed this young jungle girl to find a piece of a mirror in the jungle; and for the first time in what seemed like endless years, she saw herself in the reflection of that mirror. The little girl in mirror she saw that day changed her life in the jungle forever. She realized then that she was not the same as her monkey family who adopted her with whom she had lived with all those years. She began to search for monkeys that looked like her—humans.

Then the day finally happened.

Just as the providential hand of God provided this helpless little 4-year-old girl a way of escape in that jungle through the hands of monkeys, the Lord led this now roughly 10-year-old little jungle girl a way out of that jungle through the hands of humans. God sent hunters into that area of the jungle who were looking for animals, birds and other wildlife to capture for profit. Seeing one of the hunters from atop a tall tree she was hiding in, she recognized she looked like them. This little girl climbed down; approached one of the hunters slowly on all fours as monkeys do; and humbly offered her outstretched hand to them as monkeys do in a gesture of friendship, hoping they would accept her.

The response one of the hunters gave this little girl was as glorious a moment as Christ who reached out His hand to touch the leper and said, "*I am willing*" (Matthew 8:3), or Michelangelo's painting of the finger of God touching the finger of man. The hunter's hand reached out and grasped hold of this little girl's hand in friendship and acceptance, and brought this long lost little child back to the family of humans where she belonged.

This little girl didn't have to get cleaned up before going home with these humans. She came to them just as she was with long knotted, matted hair down to her knees infested with bugs and lice, coarse and blackened skin from never having washed herself, crouched over on all fours like a monkey because she didn't know how to walk upright, and only able to make grunting sounds to communicate. It didn't matter— they knew she was one of them and accepted her just as she was.

This is what your loving heavenly Father wants to do with you. His hand is already outstretched in loving gesture to you before you even thought to stretch out your hand to Him, hoping you will recognize His love for you and take hold of His hand of friendship. Those monkeys you're hanging out with in this world—they may love you while you're doing what they're doing in this worldly jungle but that's not where you belong. It doesn't matter how bad you look; God accepts you just the way you are, covered in the knotted and matted sins of this world. You belong with the family of God. Like this little girl, you knew it in your heart the day you saw your reflection in the mirror of God's word.

If you've been dragged off by the Satan deep into the jungle of this world, separated from God or church; and you are ready to climb down from that tree and head back to where you belong with God and His people in church, reach your hand out to God with this prayer:

If you are a Christian, but are a prodigal brother or sister who drifted away from your Heavenly Father or church, and want to return home to Him again, pray this prayer:

> *"Father God, forgive me for being away from You and church. I repent of my sins and rededicate my life to you. Fill me with Your passion for You, Your house and Your people again. Give me the strength and wisdom to return to church where Your people are, and to remain and abide with You, Your house and Your people always. Help me to make You, Your house and Your people the most important priorities in my life. Give me the help I need to find a good church in my local area to attend. In Jesus name, amen."*

If you are not a Christian, pray this prayer:

> *Dear Lord Jesus, I believe You died on the cross for my sins. I confess I am a sinner and I repent of my sins and ask You to forgive me and cleanse me by Your blood You shed for me on the cross. I receive You as my Lord and Savior. Help me to make You, Your house and Your people the most important priorities in my life. Give me the help I need to find a good church in my local area to attend. Amen."*

The Loving Truth about Small Groups

In the 2018 Scripps National Spelling Bee, a 14-year-old wild-card contender from McKinney, Texas by the name of Karthik Nemmani unexpectedly won the trophy over a four-time veteran who was favored to win the spelling contest. What was the final word he had to spell in order to win? The word was "koinonia". When Karthik asked the announcer for the definition of koinonia, the announcer said, *"Intimate spiritual communion and participative sharing in a common religious commitment and spiritual community"*.

The reason this Greek word *koinonia* and its definition is important to us is because it embodies what we as Christians should be doing with other believers. As Christians, we should be seeking out intimate spiritual fellowship (communion) with other believers; we should be actively participating in sharing with other believers; we should be committed to other believers; and we should make believers part of our community of family and friends. This is the essence of Christian fellowship that helps us as Christians grow stronger spiritually through interaction with other Christians.

These elements of koinonia occur numerous times in the Bible such as the following:

"The believers continued to devote themselves to what the apostles were teaching, to fellowship, to the breaking of bread, and to times of prayer." (Acts 2:42 ISV)

"Let the word of Christ richly dwell within you as you teach and admonish one another with all wisdom, and as you sing psalms, hymns, and spiritual songs with gratitude in your hearts to God." (Colossians 3:16 ESV)

"Let us think of ways to motivate one another to acts of love and good works." (Hebrews 10:24 NLT)

As you consider these elements that embody the definition of this type of Christian fellowship called koinonia, you'll notice this level of fellowship normally does not occur within the framework of a very large church gathering. It's nearly impossible to get acquainted with people at the level required of this koinonia definition of Christian fellowship in a large church setting. Neither does koinonia work when you are watching a Christian television program or listening to Christian music, as helpful as that may be in your Christian walk. That's why it's important to seek what most churches call a "small group" because it's within a small group setting of roughly 5 to 15 people where you can experience the intimate spiritual fellowship, participative sharing, commitment and community of the koinonia type of Christian fellowship that produces a stronger, more fulfilling Christian life.

When you begin your search for a church home in your local area, always check to see if that church has any small groups that you or your family members might be interested in joining. Most church websites will have a tab or link that will say something like "Small Groups", "Belonging", "Connect", "Grow", "Next Steps", "Bible Studies", "Ministries" or "Serve" that will provide you their list of small groups. It is even more important to do this when the church has 500 people or more in attendance. It is these small groups that will help make a church, particularly large churches, seem much smaller, friendlier and easier to get to know people on a more personal level.

The people you will most likely become closest to within any church are the people in your small group of that church. Oftentimes, being part of a small group within a church will give you and your family members the support and encouragement to join in other activities within that church. An added bonus of small groups is it is sometimes easier to invite someone you know to a small group instead of a larger church service—an excellent way to introduce them to other people in your church; and you'll be helping another person return home to their loving heavenly Father.

Many churches are also eager to let you to start your own small group if you have a Bible study or subject, hobby, passion, recreation, sport, community outreach or other interest that you enjoy that currently does not already exist as a small group at that church. Do you enjoy cruising on your motorcycle on weekends? Start a motorcycle small group. Do you enjoy nature walks, bike riding, mountain climbing, Parkour, Tough Mudder or CrossFit? Start a small group for people with similar outdoor or indoor interests. Do you enjoy knitting and crocheting? How about starting a small group for people who enjoy your same interests? Do you like Bible studies in homes or in an available room at the church? Go for it!—start one. Do you like volunteering at a local food bank, homeless shelter or nursing home for the elderly in your city? Why not start a small group of people who can serve the community with you? There's no end to the type of small groups you can start or be involved in to help yourself and other people get more involved and engaged with one another. Make your large church more inviting, approachable and welcoming through small groups.

When I was attending Grace Church in Maryland Heights, Missouri pastored by Ron Tucker, among all the wonderful things this pastor and church did for their members and their surrounding community, they also provided many types of small groups for people to join. They created a large variety of small groups to meet different desires and needs of their members: groups based on age, hobbies, interests, struggles, passions to serve, careers, etc.

One of the small groups I joined at this church was a group that took trips to the poorest locations in Mexico to build small, simple homes for many poor families that were living in tiny makeshift shacks they built by hand from tin and wood they found in their city trash landfill where they were living in the worst of conditions. Another small group I joined was a group of construction workers and non-construction volunteers like me that did free repairs on homes of low income, elderly and disabled families around the local city of St. Louis. Although the members of this church numbered in the thousands, in these small groups, I experienced my greatest Christian growth through the intimate and spiritual fellowship, participative sharing, commitment and community that this koinonia type of Christian fellowship requires.

Another great tool Pastor Tucker used to help every member of Grace Church grow spiritually through connecting together in small groups was challenge each member of Grace Church to use the book "*Better Together: What on earth are we here for?*" by Pastor Rick Warren. This is a "*40 Days of Community*" workbook that small groups can use for discussion and actions to help everyone in their groups understand and develop the elements of koinonia. To help promote and facilitate the koinonia type of Christian fellowship, the *Better Together* workbook explains how we grow better together, serve better together, worship better together, and reach out better together. I highly recommend Pastor Warren's book for those churches and small groups looking for a good book to use for your small group discussions.

The Prodigal Son is a Spectator, Not a Team Player

Christianity is more like a team sport and less like an individual sport. Christianity was meant to be lived out together among other believers to win in life on the great harvest field of mankind the way a soccer team at the World Cup, football team at the Super Bowl or baseball team at the World Series was meant to be played out among other players on their team in order to win in sports on the field together. Perhaps the reason Christianity is losing on the fields of America—in education, in politics, in business, in media and entertainment, in sports, in society issues and family matters—is because Christians are trying to win on their own (alone) instead of together as a group, a team, a united body of Christ.

Everyone wants to be the Lone Ranger but don't forget that even the Lone Ranger needed Tonto to win his battles too. Just look at what happened in this last presidential election when Christians united their votes together in politics—Trump was elected! Ok, I realize if you didn't vote for President Trump, you probably cringed at these words but the fact remains that it took a united effort of Christians coming out in mass that helped get Donald Trump elected as our nation's 45th president; and that is what it's going to take—Christians united as a team—that will help get President Trump reelected to a second term. Dr. Lance Wallnau, one of only three evangelical leaders to accurately predict Trump's presidential win, stated, "*It was the Christian turnout at the last minute*" that won the 5 swing states that got Trump elected president.

The mainstream media already understands this teamwork strategy. That's why they're colluding together in concerted effort as a team with leaked classified information from people within government, fake news, deceptive reporting and one-sided talk shows to oppose Trump and his administration. To their credit, mainstream media understands the concept of teamwork in the affairs of this world more than the people of God. Even Jesus revealed that the people of this world are more astute, clever and savvy than Christians when it comes to the affairs of this world when He said, "*It is true that the children of this world are more shrewd in dealing with the world around them than are the children of the light.*" (Luke 16:8 NLT) The media, Hollywood elitists, liberal politicians, left-wing professors and revisionist historians are all shrewdly working together as a team to eliminate our Christian culture in America.

It's time we Christians rise up again like those dead bones that the prophet Ezekiel spoke to that rose from the dead. (Ezekiel 37) Some of you are asking, "*Can these dry bones of Christianity in America live?*" I'm going to speak a prophecy over the dead bones of Christianity in America the way the prophet Ezekiel spoke over those dead bones in his day: I prophesy over the dead bones of Christianity in America, and I say to these dead bones: "*Dry bones, hear the word of the LORD! This is what the Sovereign LORD says to these bones: 'I will make breath enter you, and you will come to life. I will attach tendons to you and make flesh come upon you and cover you with skin; I will put breath in you, and you will come to life. Then you will know that I am the LORD.'*" (Ezekiel 37:4–6 NIV) Amen!"

Like Jake Sully spoke to his Na'vi people on the land of Pandora in the movie, *Avatar*, I'm speaking to Christians in the land of America today saying, "*The ungodly people in America have sent us Christians a message: 'That they can take whatever they want in our nation—our families, children and educational system, our sports, media and entertainment, our businesses and politics, our culture, freedom of speech and religion. That no one can stop them.' Well we Christians will send them a message. You ride out as fast as the breath of God can carry you. You tell the other clans of Christians to come. Tell them Christ calls to them! You fly now with me on the wings of the Lord! My brothers in Christ! Sisters in Christ! And we will show the ungodly people in America that they cannot take whatever they want! And that this nation is our land, one nation under God, a Christian nation!*" It was in 1892 that the United States Supreme Court ruled that "*This is a Christian Nation*", and this ruling issued by Associate Justice David Brewer has never been legally disputed or overturned in the history of our nation, nor shall it ever be overturned. So stand up Christians in America! Be a team player on God's team; not a spectator watching from a distance.

Another reason Christianity in America has lost its battle on the field of politics, business, education, media and entertainment, in sports, society issues and family matters is because Christian programming, churches, organizations and plain old grassroots Christianity in America lacks that shrewd grit that the mainstream media is using against Donald Trump. Christianity somewhere along the way gave up, threw in the towel and gave in to the ungodly in our nation; whereas you'll notice that the ungodly in our nation never seem to give up at standing up, speaking out and churning out more ungodliness in our nation.

Christianity in America needs to regrow its backbone to rise up— every Christian, church, ministry and organization as one team, one body in Christ with one purpose and mind in Christ to take back our nation for Christ. Every Christian in America needs to promote, educate and encourage other Christians in America to get involved in education, politics, business, media and entertainment, in sports, and society issues that affect the everyday lives of Americans. For too long, Christians in America have shrunk back more and more into the shadows of passivity; giving in to the peer pressure of political correctness and the status quo; choosing the cowardice of silence rather than standing together to be the bold and loud voice of conscience and godly change for our nation. It's time we Christians take action to change our nation, our education system, our political system, our business sectors, our sports, media and entertainment platforms, and our culture and conscience for God's kingdom instead of watching our prodigal nation fall over the cliff into the swine pit of destruction.

That's what our founding fathers did for our nation. In 1776, in the face of pressures of war with Great Britain, our Second Continental Congress in Philadelphia united together as one bold and loud voice of conscience and godly change for our United States that produced the Declaration of Independence that was adopted by Congress on July 4, 1776. The rest is history as we very well know.

The words at the top of the Declaration of Independence read: "*The unanimous Declaration of the thirteen United States of America*". Did you get that? They said, "*unanimous Declaration*"; not "half of us Declaration" or "one-fourth of us Declaration" or the "Protestants but not the Catholics Declaration". They were all declaring loud and proud and fully in agreement with one another. That's what the Christians, churches, ministries and organizations in America need to do today. Whatever label your Christianity goes by—Protestants, Catholics, Baptists, Presbyterians, Methodists, non-denominational, inter-denominational and everyone else who calls themselves "Christian", we need to declare unanimously, fully in agreement, united in one accord with everyone onboard that our nation will be *one nation UNDER GOD, indivisible, with justice and liberty for all* as our Pledge of Allegiance to our flag and nation once stated. Simply put: One team of Christianity in America to take on anyone and anything on the field of American soil that comes against us. It's time we take back our nation for Christ!

One way we Christians can unite together as one bold and loud voice of conscience and godly change for our nation in order to take back our nation for Christ is to get registered to vote and then go out and vote at every possible election. A 2016 Barna Group survey of American voters during our 2016 presidential election revealed "religious beliefs" have the greatest influence on voting decisions and their choice for president. Among those voters, 75% evangelicals assigned "a lot of influence" to their religious beliefs in their voting decisions compared to 30% non-evangelical born again Christians; 18% of other non-Christian faiths; and 5% of religious skeptics (atheists, agnostics or no religious affiliations). Nearly half of the evangelical and born again Christian categories under 50 years old stated their religious beliefs had "a lot of influence" in their voting decisions compared to one-third of those in these two categories over age 50. That's the good news among voting Christians.

However, the bad news is evangelical and born again Christians aren't engaged in the political process. According to the 2016 Barna survey, "*evangelical Christians were actually the faith group least engaged with the presidential race, despite the fact they were the religious segment most likely to characterize the outcome of this year's presidential election as extremely important to the future of the United States."*

There are roughly 60 million evangelicals in America today—that can make a huge difference in the political process and the November 2018 midterm elections for seats in Congress that will have the greatest impact on helping or hurting President Trump's administration; and yet, roughly 24 million (40%) of evangelicals are not even registered to vote. In the 2000 presidential election, only 15 million evangelicals voted. When evangelical leaders urged voters to register and vote in the 2004 presidential election, 28.9 million evangelicals voted, but this is still a shamefully low turnout when considering there are 60 million evangelicals in America. In 2018, David Barton, the evangelical Christian political activist, historian, author and founder of WallBuilders, said on the Daystar television network that during the 2016 presidential election, there were *"55 million professing Christians who did not vote."* And you wonder why our country is in the mess it's in. It's because Christians in America have buried their head along with their vote in the sand instead of using their vote to change the course of our nation for God.

All Christians must once again get informed, educated and engaged in the political process if we expect to turn our nation's capital, our nation's laws and our nation's people back toward Christ. God has given Christians tremendous power to do so by giving us voting power; if we would only wake up and see this power God has placed in our hands and use it. The Bible says, *"Therefore, whoever knows the right thing to do, yet fails to do it, is guilty of sin."* (James 4:17 BSB) Whether its Federal elections such as the presidential or congressional elections, or state and local elections such as state primaries, you have a Christian responsibility to be involved in shaping our nation for Christ through your vote and involvement in the political process. Get registered and vote Christian!

Three websites to help you make informed voting decisions are Truth & Liberty Coalition at truthandliberty.net, WallBuilders at wallbuilders.com and the American Culture & Faith Institute at culturefaith.com. These websites provide many resources about God in politics and will help inform and educate you about Federal, state and local voting. Former TV star Kirk Cameron's website TheCourage.com is filled with inspiring, encouraging, fun and challenging content that helps restore the cultural landscape of America. Cameron said, "*We believe it's time for Christians to have the courage to be countercultural, while maintaining a posture of humility*"; and during a live event attended by more than 150,000 people, Cameron urged "*people of faith to return to biblical principles and to get involved in the election season.*"

Another easy way for Christians to get involved in the political process to shape our nation for good is by signing petitions online. For example, when you receive an email to sign a petition to protect the right to life for unborn children, you should sign that petition. You don't have to give any money to these organizations presenting the petition; all you have to do is simply sign their petition by typing in your name and email address and then click the "Sign" button—that's it! This is one of the best ways your voice can be heard in Washington along with other Christians who are impacting our nation's political process by influencing Trump's administration and Congress. One place where you can find petitions that support Christian causes in America is the American Center for Law & Justice (ACLJ) at https://aclj.org/petitions. Want to see more petitions to sign? Click the "More Petitions" button at this website. Better yet, sign up at the ACLJ website to receive any new petitions to sign via email on subjects that have an impact on our Christian culture in America.

Satan is the one who is deceiving and misguiding Christians into thinking they should not be involved in the political process. If Christians do not get involved in politics, then the only people left voting, filling political positions and making crucial moral decisions for our nation are the ungodly who want to change our nation into an immoral nation that is against God; a nation that opposes all things that God and Christianity stand for; and a nation of evil whose sins and disobedience will result in God's punishment and destruction of our nation. Dietrich Bonhoeffer said it best when he said, "*Silence in the face of evil is itself evil: God will not hold us guiltless. Not to speak is to speak. Not to act is to act.*"

What you are starting to see today with Christian ministers once again having access to the White House through President Trump's administration is Christians doing what they were called to do by Almighty God all along—occupying and doing business until Jesus returns. (Luke 19:13) The idea of religious leaders at the side of political leaders should not be so surprising to you if you read your Bible because God always had prophets that counseled kings who were the politicians of their day throughout Bible times. If God is involved in politics, so should you. Even the antichrist who will be a political figure in the Last Days will have his religious leader at his side—the false prophet, also known as the second beast in the Bible. (Revelation 13:11–17, 19:20)

While Daniel was in captivity in Babylon, he prophesied of the End Times in which we are in; times where wickedness is running rampant and the antichrist is soon to be revealed. In Daniel's prophecy, he spoke of the character of the people of God who will stand up and take action against the flattery, seduction and corruption of Satan in education, in politics, in business, in media and entertainment, in sports, in society issues and family matters. Daniel said, *"He [Satan] shall seduce with flattery those who violate the covenant [of God], but the people who know their God shall stand firm and take action."* (Daniel 11:32 ESV, bracketed emphasis mine) What you are seeing today at the White House is Christianity waking up and realizing its rightful place in politics. People who know their God—Christian ministers—are standing firm and taking action in the White House to be that bold and loud voice of conscience and godly change for our nation.

This is not only happening in politics; it's happening in other areas as well, such as in the media and entertainment. Why do you suppose there are more Christian films being produced in our generation, such as *The Passion, The Chronicles of Narnia, End of the Spear, Fireproof, Courageous* and *Paul, Apostle of Christ*? You're also seeing an uptick of Christian personalities using their platform in entertainment to tell people about Christ, such as pastor John Gray in *The Book of John Gray* reality show on the Oprah Winfrey Network; and Chris Pratt, the leading star in the *Guardians of the Galaxy* and *Jurassic World* films, who told young people about God's love and grace in his thank-you speech when accepting the *MTV*'s 2018 Generation Award. These are people who know their God and their rightful place in the media and entertainment sector who are standing firm and taking action to be that bold and loud voice of conscience and godly change for our nation.

The same thing is happening in sports. Never before have athletes been more vocal in using their platform in sports for the glory of God. After the underdog Philadelphia Eagles won the 2018 NFL Super Bowl LII against the favored to win New England Patriots, their quarterback and MVP of the game, Nick Foles, was quick to give all the glory to God at the podium for their Super Bowl victory. What was Nick doing? He was using his platform in sports to be that bold and loud voice of conscience and godly change for our nation. When the Eagles Head Coach, Doug Pederson, was asked at the Super Bowl podium, *"How do you explain this that 9 years ago you're coaching in high school and here you are with this trophy?"* Doug didn't hesitate with a bold and loud voice of Christian conscience in saying, *"I can only give the praise to my Lord and Savior Jesus Christ for giving me this opportunity."*

As we enter the Last Days on God's calendar, now is not the time to isolate and separate yourself from God and His people—the church. Now is the hour for Christians everywhere to stand up, speak up, speak out and be counted among the people of God who will realize their calling from God, show their faith by their action and take their rightful place in church, in education, in politics, in business, in media and entertainment, in sports, and in society issues and family matters.

God does not operate like the CIA or a clandestine operation. God is not impressed with or interested in closet Christians, secret agent saints or double agent disciples. God wants Christians who will stand shoulder to shoulder with other Christians in public, fully clothed in the fellowship of Jesus Christ for all eyes to see. Don't let Satan fool you into thinking you are fully clothed in God's purpose for your life when you actually appear shamefully naked of any sort of connection and involvement with God's people and God's purpose for your life in our nation and the world.

I'm not saying it's wrong to watch your favorite minister or church service on TV or online in the privacy of your home. I enjoy watching and listening to my favorite Christian ministers, church services, Christian music and other Christian programming on TV, online and radio too. In fact, each week without fail I'm watching or listening to Christian programming on TV, online or radio whether it's someone teaching the word of God, a televised Christian program or Christian music at home or in my car. I'm not encouraging you or me to stop doing those things. Keep enjoying those things but don't use those things to replace or substitute for *physically* being in church with God's people, the body of Christ, and taking part in Christian causes and activities that change the course of our nation and world for Christ. Don't become comfortable and content with just watching and listening to the things of God from a distance like a spectator watching a sporting event—be there in person on the field as a player for God's team! That's the true Christian experience.

Are You the Prodigal Son or the Prodigal Son's Brother?

Although we always focus on the prodigal son in Jesus' parable of the prodigal son, there were two sons in this story—the prodigal son and the prodigal son's brother. Jesus' parable of the prodigal son given to the crowd in Luke 15:25–30 was also a story about the prodigal son's brother. Jesus shares how the prodigal son's brother reacted to the prodigal son's return home by saying, "*Now his older son* [the prodigal son's brother] *was in the field. And as he came and drew near to the house, he heard music and dancing. So he called one of the servants and asked what these things meant. And he said to him, 'Your brother* [the prodigal son] *has come, and because he* [the prodigal son's father] *has received him safe and sound, your father has killed the fatted calf.' But he* [the prodigal son's brother] *was angry and would not go in. Therefore his father came out and pleaded with him. So he answered and said to his father, 'Lo, these many years I have been serving you; I never transgressed your commandment at any time; and yet you never gave me a young goat, that I might make merry with my friends. But as soon as this son of yours came, who has devoured your livelihood with harlots, you killed the fatted calf for him.'"* (Luke 15:25–30 NKJV, bracketed emphasis mine)

If you examine both of these brothers closely, you'll notice that the prodigal son's brother was exactly like the prodigal son before he left his father's house. The prodigal son and the prodigal son's brother both had the same type of heart. The problem was both sons had the wrong type of soil in their heart when the seed of their father's word fell upon it. They both were self-righteous and disobedient. They both wanted more and both thought they deserved more from their father. The only real difference between the prodigal son and the prodigal son's brother is that the prodigal son revealed his true heart's condition at the beginning of Jesus' parable, and later learned his lesson and repented; the prodigal son's brother never learned his lesson, nor did he repent, and revealed his true heart's condition at the end of Jesus' parable.

The prodigal son became humbled over time through adversity—his pride, arrogance and disobedience were broken; he repented of his self-righteousness and disobedience and returned home. The prodigal son no longer wanted more or thought he deserved more. In fact, he now knew he deserved much less than his father's son—just like one of his father's servants. And yet, his loving father forgave him of his sins completely and unconditionally and treated him as one of his sons.

The prodigal son's brother, on the other hand, still needed to learn his lesson. He was still prideful, arrogant and disobedient. He believed he deserved more when in fact all that his loving father had was already his. The Apostle Paul addressed the prodigal son's brothers in the church when he said, *"Let no one boast in men. For all things are yours: whether Paul or Apollos or Cephas, or the world or life or death, or things present of things to come—all are yours. And you are Christ's, and Christ is God's."* (1 Corinthians 3:21–23 NKJV) The prodigal son's brother did not repent of his self-righteousness, arrogance or disobedience; therefore, his sin remained in him.

The prodigal son was now working for his father with a heart of humility and gratitude after returning home. The prodigal son's brother was still working for his father with a heart of disdain, disrespect and disobedience, though he never left home. The prodigal son was blinded by his pride in the past but now he could see clearly when he returned home. The prodigal son's brother thought he could see clearly but he was blinded by his pride of his past achievements because he never left home.

The prodigal son was no longer judging his father, judging his brother or judging his place and position in his father's house; he was only judging himself now. The prodigal son's brother was still judging his father; judging his brother; and judging his place and position in his father's house. The only person the prodigal son's brother wasn't judging was himself; therefore, the judgment of his own sins remained. The Bible says, *"If we judged ourselves truly, we would not be judged"*. (I Corinthians 11:31 ESV)

This is the problem with the brothers and sisters of the prodigal son in churches today—they're always judging other people, condemning other people and despising other people. They're the gossipers, the whisperers, the finger-pointers, the frowners, the despisers, the separators, the agitators, the un-forgivers and the haters; and their judgmental attitude and behavior is always directed at whoever they think is the prodigal son.

Jesus told us about these self-righteous judgmental brothers and sisters of the prodigal son when He told the parable of the Pharisee (the brother of the prodigal son) and the tax collector (the prodigal son). First, Jesus reveals the arrogance of the "attitude of the brother of the prodigal son" in the Pharisee when Jesus said, *"To some who were confident of their own righteousness and looked down on everyone else, Jesus told this parable: Two men went up to the temple to pray, one a Pharisee and the other a tax collector. The Pharisee stood by himself and prayed: 'God, I thank you that I am not like other people—robbers, evildoers, adulterers—or even like this tax collector. I fast twice a week and give a tenth of all I get.'"* (Luke 18:9–12 NIV)

Then Jesus explains the "prodigal son's attitude" in the tax collector who has returned to God's house. Jesus said, *"But the tax collector stood at a distance. He would not even look up to heaven, but beat his breast and said, 'God, have mercy on me, a sinner.'"* (Luke 18:13 NIV)

Remember: The way you treat your brother or sister in Christ is the way you treat Jesus. Therefore, Jesus tells us how God views the prodigal son and the prodigal son's brother when He said, *"I tell you that this man* [the tax collector], *rather than the other* [the Pharisee], *went home justified before God. For all those who exalt themselves will be humbled, and those who humble themselves will be exalted."*(Luke 18:14 NIV, bracketed emphasis mine)

The way the repentant prodigal son was now treating his father's house and his father's children when he came home—with dignity, honor and respect—was the way he was now treating his father because his father's children and his father are **one**. The way the prodigal son's brother was now treating his father's house and his father's children—the prodigal son who came home—with disdain, dishonor and disrespect was the way he was now treating his father because his father's children and his father are **one**. The Apostle Paul said, *"Be kindly affectionate to one another with brotherly love, in honor giving preference to one another."* (Romans 12:10 NKJV)

Are you starting to get it? Your heavenly Father and His house and His children—the church—are **one**. From God's perspective, the way you treat the one (brothers and sisters in Christ) is the way you treat the Other (Jesus and the Father). The way you treat the church (the bride of Christ) is the way you treat the Bridegroom Jesus—there's no difference in God's eyes. Jesus said it best when He said, *"Truly I tell you, whatever you did not do for one of the least of these, you did not do for Me."* (Matthew 25:45 NIV) What this verse tells us is that the way we treat others is the way we're treating Jesus. The way we speak to other people is the way we're speaking to Jesus. The way we're judging others is the way we're judging Jesus. The way we're looking at other people is the way we're looking at Jesus. The Apostle Paul put it this way: *"When you sin like this against brothers and sisters and wound their weak conscience, you are sinning against Christ."* (1 Corinthians 8:12 CSB) Isn't it time you and I started seeing Jesus in other people?

While King David was repenting and acknowledging his sins before God for committing adultery with Bathsheba and for murdering her husband Uriah, David said in his prayer to God, "*Against You* [God]*, You only, have I sinned and done what is evil in Your sight; so You are right in Your verdict* [of me] *and justified when You judge* [me]*.*" (Psalm 51:4 NIV, bracketed emphasis mine) Wait a minute! David just committed adultery and plotted and killed an innocent man to steal his wife. Shouldn't David have said, "*Against You* [God] *and against Uriah and against Bathsheba I have sinned and done what is evil*"? If David had said it this way, it would have been redundant because David already knew when he sinned against Uriah and Bathsheba; he was actually sinning against God because God and His people are **one**. David wasn't being remiss of the fact that he committed adultery with another man's wife and murdered the husband to cover his tracks. David was simply acknowledging the fact that the way he treated God's children was the way he was treating God.

In the same way, when we tell the church, "*I want nothing to do with you*", we are actually telling God to His face, "*I want nothing to do with You*". When we say, "*The church is filled with nothing but hypocrites*", we are actually telling God to His face, "*You're a hypocrite*". When we say we're too busy for church, we're actually telling God to His face, "*I'm too busy to spend time with You*". When we make church a low priority, we've made Jesus a low priority. If we are not committed to church, we are not committed to Jesus. When we decide to leave the church, we've actually decided to leave God. When we separate and cut ourselves off from church, we've actually separated and cut ourselves off from Jesus the Vine. When we judge or hate or ridicule or gossip about or avoid or mistreat our brother or sister in Christ, we are actually judging, hating, ridiculing, gossiping about, avoiding and mistreating Jesus. It was Jesus who said, "*I tell you the truth, when you did it to one of the least of these my brothers and sisters, you were doing it to Me.*" (Matthew 25:40 NLT)

Jesus could have just told a parable about one son—the prodigal son—but He chose to mention two sons in this story in order to make this point: every person is either the prodigal son on the run; the prodigal son who returned home; or the prodigal son's brother.

Which son are you?

Let me help you with that answer: All of us were the prodigal son at one point or another. Are you having trouble seeing yourself as the prodigal son? If your reaction is like the religious Pharisees of Jesus' day who proclaimed, *"Are we blind too?"*, let me give you the answer Jesus gave those religious people in John 9:41: *"If you were blind, you would not be guilty of sin; but now that you claim you can see, your guilt remains."* In other words, if we were the prodigal son and know it, we would not be guilty of the sin of the prodigal son's brother.

The truth is we were all born as prodigal children after Adam and Eve sinned in the Garden of Eden. The Apostle Paul in the book of Romans says we were born sinners (Romans 3:9, 5:12, 5:18–19); none of us were born righteous. Even King David, the man after God's own heart, acknowledged without reservation, *"I was born a sinner—yes, from the moment my mother conceived me."* (Psalm 51:5 NLT) The NET Bible renders David's words this way: *"I was guilty of sin from birth, a sinner the moment my mother conceived me."* Pastor Robert Morris of Gateway Church in Texas goes so far as to say not only were we born with a sin nature because Adam and Eve sinned; we were born with a satanic nature because Satan was the first to sin against God—and we sided with Satan in the Garden of Eden through Adam and Eve. The Bible clearly says, *"there is no one righteous, not even one"* (Romans 3:10 NIV) and *"all have sinned and fall short of the glory of God, and all of us are justified freely by His grace through the redemption that came by Christ Jesus"*. (Romans 3:23–24 NIV)

This is why self-righteous judgmental brothers and sisters of the prodigal son have no right to judge someone else. That's Jesus' job description; not yours, not mine. The Apostle Paul put it this way:

"Therefore do not pronounce judgment before the time, before the Lord comes, who will bring to light the things now hidden in darkness and will disclose the purposes of the heart. Then each one will receive his commendation from God." (1 Corinthians 4:5 ESV) Paul continues by saying, *"For what gives you the right to make such a judgment* [against your brother]*? What do you have that God hasn't given you? And if everything you have is from God, why boast as though it were not a gift?"* (1 Corinthians 4:7 NLT, bracketed emphasis mine)

So what's the cure for all the prodigal son's brothers and sisters out there with their self-righteous judgmental spirit? When these brothers and sisters of the prodigal son prematurely judge someone of doing wrong, speaking wrong, thinking wrong or living wrong; they need to relax and just tell themselves, *"I'm no better"*, because we're all sinners by nature. That's what the Apostle Paul was doing when he said, *"Here is a trustworthy saying that deserves full acceptance: Christ Jesus came into the world to save sinners—of whom I am the worst."* (1 Timothy 1:15 NIV) If we have a problem saying *"I'm no better"* as Paul did, that is a clear sign we are the self-righteous judgmental prodigal son's brother.

We were all born as sinners. To be born a sinner means you were born unrighteous and unacceptable to God—that's something you inherited from Adam and Eve after they sinned in the Garden of Eden. The Bible tells us that *"sin entered the world through one man* [Adam], *and death* [entered the world] *through sin, and in this way death came to all people."* (Romans 5:1 NIV, bracketed emphasis mine) That's the reason why no one can make it into the kingdom of God or heaven based on their own merits or efforts. That's the bad news.

The good news is Jesus now owns the keys to death and hell (Revelation 1:18); and Jesus now uses those keys to unlock for us His new way to get into the kingdom of God through our new nature of righteousness we receive simply by faith in Jesus Christ. Jesus said, *"Unless you are born again, you cannot see the Kingdom of God."* (John 3:3 NLT) Now that we have this new nature of righteousness in Christ, we are holy, righteous and acceptable in God's sight—that's what gets us into heaven and allows us to clearly see the Kingdom of God in Christ.

The Apostle Paul said, *"Therefore, since we have been justified through faith, we have peace with God through our Lord Jesus Christ."* (Romans 5:1 NIV) Since we can't work for this new nature of righteousness, we must simply receive it freely by faith in God's grace. The Apostle Paul spoke about getting into heaven by God's grace instead of our own works when he said, *"So then, it does not depend on human will or effort but on God who shows mercy."* (Romans 9:16 HCSB)

If you think God is being unfair because He's allowing people into heaven based solely on His grace instead of people's deeds, God has an answer for you when He says, *"I will have mercy on whomever I will have mercy, and I will have compassion on whomever I will have compassion."* (Romans 9:15 NKJV) In other words, God is telling us, *"This is My heaven and My kingdom, and I'll let in it whomever I want based on whatever standard I want—and I want entrance into My heaven and My kingdom to be grace-based instead of works-based."* This way, no one can boast about themselves and what they did to get into heaven. The only thing you can boast about when it comes to getting into heaven is boasting about the goodness and grace of God. Paul makes this even clearer when he said, *"Can we boast, then, that we have done anything to be accepted by God? No, because our acquittal is not based on obeying the law* [the Ten Commandments]. *It is based on faith."* (Romans 3:27 NLT, bracketed emphasis mine)

This new nature of righteousness is not based on anything we've done. When the Bible said there is none righteous, it meant no one is righteous by actions or performance, by wealth or influence, by social status or pedigree, by giving or sacrifice, by Bible reading or worship, by serving or volunteering, by actions or attitude, or by prayers or church attendance. All of these things are a much lower bar than the one God uses to establish righteousness. The bar God uses for establishing righteousness is the beams of the cross that His own Son Jesus died on to give us His righteousness found only in Christ. Only Christ can make us righteous; and Jesus does this by giving us His nature of righteousness when we freely receive God's abundance of grace and accept His free gift of righteousness found only in Christ. (Romans 5:15–17)

168

When God sees you in Christ, He sees His own righteousness—the righteousness of Christ. You have no righteousness outside of Christ. All your righteousness is as filthy rags Isaiah 64:6 tells us. Only God's righteousness exists; there is no other righteousness outside of God in Christ. Someone can claim to be less of a sinner than me but no one can claim to be more righteous than me no matter how much good they do because our righteousness comes from Christ alone; not from ourselves.

That word "righteous" is only reserved for God who alone is righteous. That's why Jesus said, "Why do you call Me good [righteous]? No one is good [righteous] except God alone." (Mark 10:18, Luke 18:19 ESV) Jesus Himself goes so far as to say no one else is "good"; not just no one else is "righteous". In other words, Jesus was saying everyone else is "bad". Only God is good. We need God's "good" to become good. We need God's righteousness to become righteous.

Therefore, none of us are any better (more good, righteousness) than another person. You can claim to be less of a sinner but you are still a sinner nonetheless in and of yourself. You cannot take any credit for your righteousness because it is not your own; it is God's righteousness imputed to you. The prophet Isaiah tells us, "*We are all infected and impute with sin. When we display our righteous deeds, they are nothing but filthy rags.*" (Isaiah 64:6 NLT) Our own righteousness has always been as filthy rags and always will be as filthy rags. Our own righteousness will always be stained, tainted and corrupted with sin not just because of our own sins we've committed, but because of the sin we inherited from Adam and Eve. Any time we go back to trusting in our own righteousness, we go back to trusting in the sin of Adam and Eve because our own righteousness is corrupted with their sin in Eden.

Our prayer to God should be, "*Restore to us our first love!*" In other words, our prayer to God should be, "*Restore to us the wisdom, knowledge, understanding and power of Your grace! Open our eyes to see we have no righteousness apart from You O God.*"

And yet, we who are the prodigal son's brother or sister compare ourselves one to another as if our own efforts and performance measure up to be better than someone else's; and we think we are somehow better than others when all along *"we are no better than others"*. We're still just as unrighteousness as everyone else without Christ's righteousness that God freely gives to us. The more we think we are more righteous than others, the filthier our own righteousness becomes in God's sight. The more we think we are better than others, the worse we become in God's sight. The more holy we think we are than others, the more unholy we appear in God's sight. The more we see our own righteousness, the more God sees our sin. No one can claim to be more righteous than another person because all of our own righteousness stinks in the nostrils of God. It is the stench of wallowing in the swine pit of sin and disobedience like the prodigal son. (Luke 15:15)

If we say or think we've never been a prodigal son; then guess which brother we are? We're the prodigal son's brother. We're that self-righteous brother who said he never sinned against his Father; never ran away from his Father; never wasted the gifts and talents that his Father gave him and entrusted to him; and has served his Father faithfully all the time.

Every one of us has been prodigal at one point in our life. There is a time in each person's life when we do not know Christ personally. It is during this time that we are prodigal and don't know it. There is also a time in our Christian life when we know Christ but are running away from God or have chosen to separate and isolate ourselves from church. This too is a time when we are prodigal and don't even know it. The fact of the matter is every Christian has had a prodigal phase in their life when they didn't know Jesus; wasn't interested in Jesus; didn't want Jesus; wasted what Jesus was giving them in life; or was running from Jesus or His church. For me, it wasn't just one time; it was several times that I became that prodigal son, just as the recurring dreams God gave me ahead of time revealed to me. Then there was a point in our lives when we came to our senses through the help of the Holy Spirit. We realized we needed Christ and we came home to our loving Father God through the forgiveness all of us receive through faith in Jesus Christ and His blood He shed on the cross that cleanses us from all our sins.

The prodigal son's brother is a religious person who thinks he or she does not fit the profile of a prodigal son. Since this religious person is someone who is most likely going to church, reads their Bible, prays to God, and is involved in some type of religious activity, they don't see "prodigal" anywhere in their spiritual profile. When they look at the man in the mirror, all they see is someone who has always had a relationship with God and His people; never avoided church or ran away from God; always prays and reads their Bible; and is always prepared to give or serve in the community—just like the Pharisee saw himself in Jesus' parable. (Luke 18:11–12)

The problem with this self-righteous prideful attitude is that these religious people become puffed up with pride when it comes to the way they view other Christians who are struggling, disconnected or absent from church. They see themselves somehow better or more spiritual or faithful than their Christian brothers and sisters who don't have it together; who are not attending church; or who have now come back to church after being away for a time. When a prodigal brother or sister returns home to church, the prodigal son's brother forgets that they themselves were once prodigal too. As a result, these self-righteous Christians do not treat their prodigal brother or prodigal sister with the same love, compassion and open arms that their loving Father God does when that prodigal son or daughter returns home to church. The prodigal son's brother doesn't want to rejoice and celebrate his brother's return back to God's house the same way his heavenly Father God is celebrating his brother's return home. Jesus said, *"There will be more rejoicing in heaven over one sinner who repents than over ninety-nine righteous persons who do not need to repent."* (Luke 15:7 NIV) The prodigal son's brother has an angry frown on his face while the angels of God and everyone else are rejoicing over the prodigal son's return home.

So don't be surprised if you run into the prodigal son's brother when you are in church. You can't miss them. They're the ones who make you feel uncomfortable or unwelcomed. They're the ones looking down their arrogant noses at you. There the ones who would be the last to greet you or shake your hand. When you see that happening to you in church, just tell yourself, *"They're the prodigal son's brother"* and ignore them. Start connecting with those brothers and sisters in that church who know they've been prodigal just like you, and show they haven't forgotten that fact by welcoming you with open arms. If the whole entire church or the majority of people in that church make you feel uncomfortable or unwelcomed in their church, scratch that church of your list and look for another church that's filled with people who know they've been prodigal too, and show it by their love and acceptance of you just as you are. Trust me, not all churches are filled with a bunch of self-righteous prodigal son's brothers and sisters. Most of them know they are the prodigal son who has come home too—just as me.

CHAPTER FOUR

The Second Dream

Why does the eye see a thing more clearly in dreams than the imagination when awake?

Leonardo da Vinci

When two full years had passed, Pharaoh had a dream . . . He fell asleep again and had a second dream.

Genesis 41:1, 5 NIV

God's Greatest Dreams are Reserved for the Humble

God oftentimes prefers to pour His greatest gifts into the weakest and humblest of vessels because God said, *"My power is made perfect in weakness."* (1 Corinthians 12:9 ESV) God hates and despises pride, arrogance and boasting. God said, *"I hate pride and arrogance, corruption and perverse speech."* (Proverbs 8:13 NLT) It was pride, arrogance, corruption and perverse speech that caused Lucifer's fall from heaven and rebellion against God that turned him into Satan, the enemy and adversary of God. The Bible records Satan's pride and fall when it says, *"How you are fallen from heaven, O Lucifer, son of the morning! How you are cut down to the ground, you who weakened the nations! For you have said in your heart: 'I will ascend into heaven, I will exalt my throne above the stars of God; I will also sit on the mount of the congregation on the farthest sides of the north; I will ascend above the heights of the clouds, I will be like the Most High [God].' Yet you shall be brought down to Sheol, to the lowest depths of the Pit."* (Isaiah 14:12–15 NKJV, bracket emphasis mine)

God knows that Satan's primary goal is to make mankind just as prideful and arrogant as he is so that mankind will also fall from God, just as Satan persuaded Adam and Eve to do in the Garden of Eden.

Therefore, when God chooses to pour His greatest gifts into people, He oftentimes chooses the weakest, humblest, basest and most despised of people so they cannot boast in themselves. The Apostle Paul tells us, *"God has chosen the foolish things of the world to put to shame the wise, and God has chosen the weak things of the world to put to shame the things which are mighty; and the base things of the world and the things which are despised God has chosen, and the things which are not, to bring to nothing the things that are, that no flesh should glory in His presence . . . as it is written, He who glories, let him glory in the LORD."* (1 Corinthians 1:27–29, 31 NKJV)

That's how it was with Moses of whom the Bible says *Moses was a very humble man, more so than anyone on the face of the earth.* (Numbers 12:3 CSB) This former prince of Egypt became the fugitive of Egypt—he was an outcast from Egypt and from his own people the Jews; a man despised and scarred with a criminal record of murdering a man. He was running from his foolish, bad decisions and mistakes of the past. He once stood among royalty in the palace of pharaoh but now lived a humbled life for 40 years standing among sheep and goats on the backsides of a mountain far from his dreams. But this is what made Moses a ready vessel for God to pour into him God's greatest gifts to deliver the children of Israel from bondage in Egypt.

Another person who experienced life as a humbled outcast was Leonardo Da Vinci. Little known to most people, this great Renaissance dreamer of inventions, paintings, sculpting, science, music, mathematics, engineering, astronomy and other polymath gifts from God was born out of wedlock as a poor illegitimate child. In the 1400s in Italy, being an illegitimate child automatically classified you into the lower class of people in society who had no rights to property, limited education and no access to any public jobs. The only jobs given to illegitimate children during that time in Italy were servants, priests or artisans.

Leonardo was classified at the bottom of the working class, but he was another humbled vessel that God made ready to lavishly pour His greatest dreams and extravagant gifts into. After living his first five years with his mother who was a peasant, Leonardo's father took him from his mother and sent him into the artisan apprenticeship, and rarely contacted him after that. However, by the grace of God, Leonardo would go from humble beginnings to living among royalty. In fact, paintings and records show the king of France holding Leonardo's head in his arms as he died at age 67 in his residence at the Château du Clos Lucé in Amboise, France. What man tried to limit in Leonardo's life—his dreams, God turned into limitless potential and success.

But those dreams of inventions and other great gifts God gave to Leonardo was not just for his benefit alone—this too, as with so many other dreamers to whom God gives dreams, would be for the benefit of all mankind. Perhaps in all of the *Renaissance Man*'s self-learning, he discovered what other humble vessels have understood: that the reason God chooses the humblest of vessels into which to pour His greatest gifts is because God is looking for someone He can trust to hold those gifts without becoming prideful—and what better vessel than the broken, the weak and the humble. When God gives you a dream or gift, show God you can be trusted to remain a humbled vessel to hold that dream or gift; and God will give you another gift, another idea, another dream.

I Have a Second Dream

I didn't think I'd ever have another dream like those recurring dreams from God I dreamt when I was 17 years old. Over 40 years had passed since I first experienced those recurring dreams from the Lord of falling off that cliff for 7 consecutive nights. I'd completely lived out those recurring dreams in the reality of my life over a span of 40 years—just as God had shown them to me in those dream nightmares. I'd learned my life lessons of a prodigal son just as I had learned how to pop out of those dreams by not resisting and struggling with God. I was now committed to staying in God's house with His people. No more running away from God or His church—the house I saw over my right shoulder in those recurring dreams. It was over. I could go on with my life not having to worry about another terrifying fall of that dream haunting my life again because I had no intention of ever falling away from God or church ever again.

It is over, right God?

It's not over until God says it's over; and apparently, God had a new message for me and *you* through another recurring dream. In February of 2018, I had one of those repeat dreams in my sleep from God again. Just as with my previous recurring dreams from God over 40 years ago when I was 17 years old, these recurring dreams in 2018 were nightmares that had me popping out of those dreams trembling just as before. However, unlike my previous recurring dreams that I dreamt for 7 nights in a row, I dreamed only two of the exact same dream nightmares in the same night, similar to the way Pharaoh had dreamt his two dream nightmares in the same night about the 7 years of plenty and 7 years of famine (Genesis 41:1–5). I knew these were not ordinary dreams because the premonition I sensed from those two dreams about something that was going to happen in the future was just as strong of a feeling as when I dreamt those other recurring dreams four decades ago.

By this time in my life, I was 59 years old. Some would say that qualifies me as one of the *"old men who dream dreams"* spoken of in Joel 2:28–31 and Acts 2:17 of the Bible. At this point in my life, I had already learned to distinguish between normal dreams we all have and a dream that comes from God that gives you a premonition of something that is about to happen in the future.

As I fell asleep and began to dream these new recurring dreams from the Lord, I saw myself somewhere in a house. (Yes, a house was in this dream too; only this time I was in the house instead of outside running from the house because I had returned home to God's house—the church.) In my dream, I walked over to a window inside the house that had the curtains closed to look at what was outside the window. I pulled the curtain to one side to look outside the glass window, and to my horror I saw a huge wall of water heading straight in my direction. It was one gigantic, tsunami wave of water the height of which was taller than any skyscraper I'd ever seen. It was so wide that I couldn't see where either side of the giant wall of water ended. This was no small flood of water coming my way. It was an unbelievably ginormous wall of water that was about to come crashing down on me like something out of a *Deep Impact, 2012, The Day After Tomorrow* or *San Andreas* movie.

In the dream, I panicked seeing this huge wall of liquid death headed my way. I knew it was too late for me to run to higher ground. It was too late for me to pack my things. It was too late to jump in my car and drive to safety. It was too late . . . period. I decided to prepare for the inevitable death and destruction that would ensue. As ludicrous as this may sound, I started checking the front door to make sure it was locked because my plan was to ride out the rushing onslaught of this wave by staying inside the house. As the huge wall of water came crashing down, the house shook and rumbled with the force of an earthquake. The water seeping through the sides of the front door would not be denied entry.

I remember telling the people who were with me in the house (I didn't know who those people were) to get ready to escape this disaster that had overtaken us. In my frantic thinking, my plans were to open the door of this house at some point, let the water come rushing in the house and then swim out. In hindsight, this plan sounds ridiculous (but we all have dreamed more ridiculous things than this foolish plan of mine). In my dream, I remember stopping and thinking, *"I'll never get the door open because the pressure of the water will not let me open the door."* That's when the dream suddenly ended.

I awoke, startled, dazed and frightened about what I just dreamt, but relieved that it was only a dream—or was it . . . again? Like the other recurring dreams God gave me when I was 17, this dream left a strong premonition and lasting impression on my mind and within my soul; like an imprint that God wanted stamped on my mind long after I had awakened from that dream. I immediately thought about those multiple dreams I experienced when I was 17 years old and wondered to myself, *"Is God trying to tell me something about my future again?"* Relieved for the time being that it was only a dream, I let myself fall back to sleep.

Then the exact same dream repeated itself again that same night. In my dream, I was in that house again; and again I went over to the window to look outside. I drew back the curtains to look outside, and there barreling down on me was that same huge wall of water headed my way. Again I panicked, knowing it was too late to do anything to get away from that deadly wall of water. Once again my impending sense of doom swallowed me up in fear as that same mountain sized wall of water traveled closer and closer to where I was. This time, instead of trying to rescue myself with a foolish plan of opening up the door and swimming my way out of there, I immediately dropped to my knees and cried out to Jesus for help. (I learned to let go and let God.) The moment I cried out to my Lord Jesus for help, I saw that huge wall of water immediately drop straight down and disappear. I mean that huge wall of water stopped in its tracks and immediately dropped straight down and out of sight. It was as if someone had turned off the water flowing from a faucet—the water dropped that quickly in a second. I was safe. God had heard my prayer in that dream and intervened and rescued me from the onslaught of that watery death. Then I awoke from that dream again.

Once again, I realized it was only a dream—but was it? After that second repeat dream in the same night, that was the last time I dreamt that dream. I slept soundly and peacefully the rest of the night and the following nights. Was it just a dream or was it God speaking to me again like He had done at another time in my life to show me what He was about to do in my life and in the lives of other people? Was God again giving me a message in my sleep revealing to me what was about to take place in my future and the future lives of others around me? I immediately started asking God to give me the interpretation of this dream; to tell me what He wanted me to know about my future and perhaps the future of other people.

The following day, I tried retracing the steps of that dream to interpret what the dream meant. The main thought that was etched on my mind was that the huge wall of water could possibly mean a huge incoming missile strike. I also thought perhaps I was going to be somewhere on vacation near ocean water such as Hawaii; and I might get caught unawares by an oncoming tsunami. However, my mind kept going back to it possibly being an incoming nuclear missile attack. I would learn later that this interpretation was right on both counts—these dreams had something to do with both a missile strike and Hawaii.

The dream seemed so real, it had me shaking when I came out of it. *"Should I tell someone about this dream?"* I thought to myself. Believe me; I wanted to tell some people about these dreams to see what they thought about these strange recurring dreams I had. But what if these dreams turned out to be nothing? I decided I would tell no one about these two dreams I had experienced. If these dreams didn't materialize into reality in my life; and believe me, I didn't want a nuclear missile attack on our nation becoming a reality, I would not tell anyone about this dream. But if this dream became a reality in some way in my life, then I would share this dream with others.

The Second Dream Interpretation

I believe these two exact same dreams God gave me in one night was God showing me America being overwhelmed by a full-scale nuclear missile attack with multiple inbound missiles headed toward America. But God showed me previously that I could avert death and disaster to America through prayer. Earlier I told you how pharaoh of Egypt accepted Joseph's interpretation as a message from God; and he was able to avert death and disaster that was headed toward his nation in the form of 7 years of famine. Even though God may give you a dream about something that is a premonition of something to come, I've learned that you can avert or change the outcome or effect of that premonition even though those premonitions in your dreams become a reality in your life.

From that moment on, I began praying each morning specifically for our nation's protection from missile attacks, but more importantly, that we as a nation would humble ourselves before God; return to praying to God again as a nation; seek His face again as a nation; and repent from our sins as a nation again. God said in His word, *"If My people, who are called by My name, will humble themselves and pray and seek my face and turn from their wicked ways, then I will hear from heaven, and I will forgive their sin and will heal their land."* (2 Chronicles 7:14 NIV)

The Second Dream Fulfilled

In 2017, a potential missile attack from North Korea was now a reality for our nation. Repeated missile tests, including intercontinental ballistic missile tests, by North Korea produced the results they wanted. On November 29, 2017, North Korea successfully test-launched its first-ever Hwasong-15 missile, its largest and most powerful intercontinental ballistic missile (ICBM) that could carry nuclear warheads that could reach the US mainland. Kim Jong-un announced to the world that not only did they now have the capability to launch nuclear missile strikes; he also boasted that they can now reach the US mainland with intercontinental ballistic missiles loaded with nuclear warheads.

The tensions between North Korea and the US continued to escalate for months into the following year as both countries threatened each other with the use of nuclear weapons against each other. At the height of those tensions, both President Trump and Kim Jong-un would boast about whose "nuclear button" was bigger while President Trump told Kim Jong-un, *"Rocket man is on a suicide mission for himself and for his regime"*, while telling North Korea that any attack from them would be *"met with fire and fury"*, and the US would *"totally destroy"* North Korea. Kim Jong-un blasted President Trump by saying, *"I will surely and definitely tame the mentally deranged U.S. dotard with fire"* and *"a frightened dog barks louder."* The more I began paying attention to all of this news about a nuclear missile threat, the more I realized that my recurring dreams were coming true right before my eyes.

The US military increased their war game exercises around the Korean peninsula with South Korea and Japan in response to a possible attack from North Korea. Guam was preparing for a possible missile attack from North Korea, and Guam's Homeland Security Department distributed a two-page pamphlet to the island residents on how to prepare for and react to a nuclear strike from North Korea.

On January 13, 2018, shortly after 8 a.m. local time, Hawaii's Emergency Alert System and Commercial Mobile Alert System issued an alert over television, radio and cellphones of a real-world incoming missile attack from North Korea; and advised Hawaiian residents and vacationers on that Saturday morning to seek shelter from the incoming missile attack. People in Hawaii were in a state of panic, fearing for their lives as they scrambled to find safety and shelter from the incoming missile attack from North Korea. People were totally caught off guard. Many men, women and children were crying hysterically; saying their prayers as they frantically ran from beaches, huddled in fear in hotel rooms, bathtubs, garages, cars stuck in mass hysteria of traffic jams, and any other place they could find as their last place of existence on earth. Others called and texted their loved ones to say their last goodbyes.

Although it would take approximately 20 minutes for a missile from North Korea to reach Hawaii, residents and vacationers in Hawaii would have only 12 to 15 minutes left before the missile hit Hawaii once the warning alert is initially given to the public of incoming missiles. With so few minutes left to take any action, residents and vacationers in Hawaii were basically too late to go anywhere to protect themselves from the death and destruction that was about to overwhelm them—just as the high wall of water I faced in my recurring dreams. It was too late for them to find a way out of Hawaii. It was too late to catch a plane out; too late to take a boat out; nowhere to drive out; too late to swim out. It was too late because there was no way out. In the words of Gandalf as he read from that dusty, dilapidated old book found in the Dwarves underground mines of Moria just before they were to be attacked in one of *The Lord of the Rings* film series: "*We cannot get out . . . They are coming!*"

It would take 38 terrifying minutes later for a second message to go out before the public was informed that the first alarm was a false alarm. It turned out to be an unscheduled missile defense drill that someone at the Hawaii Emergency Management Agency mistakenly thought was a real-world missile attack.

The *Washington Post* reported that one man in Hawaii who was frantically driving home to spend his last moments of life with his two youngest children heard the second broadcast of the false alarm. He pulled over and cried as he broke down in tears. He said, "*I just kind of broke down at that point. It all kind of hit me in a wave, what I had just gone through."* This was the same wave I saw in my two recurring dreams.

The Outcome of the Second Dream Averted

Several months had passed since I first dreamed those multiple dreams about the wall of water, which to me at that time, now represented a full-scale nuclear attack upon our nation by North Korea. I was on my knees praying each morning for God to forgive our nation for our sins and intervene on our behalf. I continued to pray that we as a nation would humble ourselves again before God; return to praying to God again as a nation; seek His face again as a nation; and repent from our sins again as a nation.

Then the breakthrough happened!

On June 12, 2018, President Trump and North Korean leader Kim Jong-un met face-to-face on a Tuesday morning in Singapore at the North Korea-United States summit for a historic signing between the two leaders that would begin the denuclearization of the Korean Peninsula. I'm not sure which event was more of an unbelievably shocking event to Americans, the media and the world at large: an American president shaking hands with the current leader of North Korea and signing a document for complete denuclearization of the Korean peninsula; or that same American president—Donald Trump—winning the election against Hillary Clinton as the 45th President of the United States. All the missile threats came completely crashing down all at once with that signed agreement—the same way that gigantic wall of water came crashing down all at once in my dream.

I anxiously watched along with millions of other viewers around the world as a US president met a North Korean head of state for the first time in US history. As my eyes were glued to this historic event, I sensed the Holy Spirit telling me in my spirit that God heard my prayers and kept back that nuclear missile attack on America . . . for now.

I know some of you right now are thinking that what I just said is the most outlandishly arrogant thing you've heard me say in this book. How could I possibly think I had something to do with averting a nuclear missile attack on America from North Korea? I get it. I don't expect you to believe me. I'm just telling you what I experienced with God concerning the recurring dreams He, for some reason unbeknownst to me, has chosen to give me to warn me of future events. And I'm sure I wasn't the only person whom God was asking to pray these same prayers I was praying over those past few months. If any of you have been praying the same prayer as me, and are still praying these prayers for our nation as I am, let me know when writing a review about this book. I would love to hear from you.

After that historic signing at the North Korea-United States summit, I felt a complete peace over my soul that I had not felt since having those two recurring dreams. I also now know who those other people were who were with me in that house when that high wall of water was heading my way in those dreams. Those people were the people of my nation—those people in that house included *you*.

It was over . . . for now.

History Repeats Itself

History is not on our nation's side because history always repeats itself, including when it comes to nations being destroyed by God because of their sins. As God's judgment repeated itself with previous nations in our world's history, the same is expected to happen to our nation.

Do you remember the story of Jonah and Nineveh, the capital city of the Assyrian empire? (Jonah 1–4) Most of us remember this story in the Bible with a focus on Jonah's brief prodigal voyage at sea as he tries to run away from God's assignment to prophesy to the city of Nineveh about God's impending destruction of Nineveh for their sins. Most of us remember God's intervention of Jonah's rebellion with the large fish (some consider the fish to be a whale) that swallowed Jonah and later spits him out on shore; Jonah's subsequent repentance and return to God's mission to warn the people of Nineveh about God's coming judgment for their sins; and Nineveh's humble repentance that prevented God from bringing His death and destruction upon the Ninevites. That's how most of us who have read this story in the Bible remember it. What most of us don't realize is that Nineveh's repentance was only temporary. Once they dodged that bullet of God's wrath for their sins, they soon returned back to their sinful ways of living. (Nahum 1:14)

Nineveh was the ancient capital of the Assyrian empire, the same Assyrians that would later conquer the nation of Israel in 732 BC and carry them away into captivity to Assyria. It was these very people that Jonah did not want to warn of God's impending judgment for their sins during the reign of Jeroboam II of Israel (786–746 BC), just over a decade before the nation of Israel was completely destroyed by these same Assyrians.

After the Assyrians in the capital of Nineveh were assured by God that He would not destroy them after they repented, they were later used by God to completely destroy and capture the nation of Israel because of the Jew's sins against the Lord. Like America today, the Assyrians became prideful and thought God would not punish them, so they returned to their wicked ways. History and the Bible tell us that God responded to Nineveh's return to wickedness by sending the Babylonians and the Medes to completely destroy the Assyrian empire in 612 BC, a little over 100 years after God first warned the Assyrians in the capital of Nineveh that He would punish them for their sins. (Nahum 1:15, 3:1–19) The Bible warns us that *"The Lord is not slow in keeping His promise, as some understand slowness. Instead He is patient with you, not wanting anyone to perish, but everyone to come to repentance."* (2 Peter 3:9 NIV)

America – The Prodigal Nation

The same history can easily be repeated for our nation. I already shared the Barna Group statistics that clearly show each new generation in

America has become more post-Christian than the previous generation; and that our Generation Z (born between 1999 and 2015) is the first post-Christian generation in America that has more post-Christians in this generation than any other previous generation, and double the number of atheists than the number of adults in the entire American population.

The American Bible Society's annual *"State of the Bible"* survey for 2018 showed only 9% of the American population is Bible centered (i.e. having the highest view of Scripture and read it at least 4 or more times a week) compared to 54% Bible skeptics (i.e. those who believe the Bible is just another book of teachings with stories and advice) who are the largest segment of the American population. Among those 9% Americans who are Bible centered, 38% are Boomers (ages 53–71), 35% are Gen Xers (ages 34–52), and 19% are Millennials (ages 19–33). Notice the dramatic drop in percentages with each new generation in America?

What these statistics mean is that with each new generation in America, God and the Bible are becoming more and more irrelevant. With each new generation, America is falling repeatedly off that cliff and dropping further in a downward spiraling fall to its total destruction at the bottom—just like in my recurring dreams when I was 17 years old.

For Gen Zers who are Bible centered, that percentage is nearing "Z" for zero. How fitting for this youngest of our nation's generations to be labeled "Z" because, just as the last letter in the alphabet, it prophesies "the last generation" in our nation when God's patience for our nation's apostasy, disobedience and sins will have come to an end like the alphabet. (2 Peter 3:9 NIV) This labeling of our Z generation was no coincidental naming by an advertising agency; the labeling of our nation's generations is God's countdown clock for America's destruction if we do not repent and turn back to God.

This is why you can no longer trust what the American polls are telling you in terms of *"what America needs"* because America is becoming more and more an ungodly, apostate nation with each new generation. With each new generation, all the polls taken by Americans are being completed by post-Christian people more and more. In other words, the vast majority of people in America being polled by Pew

Research Center, Gallop, Barna, Statista and other pollsters are increasing becoming a majority of ungodly, post-Christian people answering these polls. Notice I didn't say these polls are telling you *"what America wants"* because we already know with each new generation, America wants less and less of God and the Bible, and more and more of Satan and sin.

We are well on our way to our own Nineveh episode of complete destruction of our nation for our sins and rebellion against God, just as the Assyrian empire. Any nation who turns its back on God will suffer. The Bible says, *"The counsel of the LORD stands forever, the plans of His heart to all generations. Blessed is the nation whose God is the LORD."* (Psalm 33:11–12 ESV) *"The wicked will go down to the grave. This is the fate of all the nations who ignore God."* (Psalm 9:17 NLT)

Many Christians, theologians, religious and nonreligious people alike have all wondered why a nation so powerful as the United States is not mentioned anywhere in Bible prophecy about the End Times, or not specifically identified in the Last Days narrative Jesus gives to the Apostle John in the book of Revelation. Could it be because America's growing apostasy will have reached its climax of God's patience with our nation's last generation in the alphabet—the Z generation?

All the research, statistics and polls from Christian and secular research and polling firms point to the United States being on track with each new generation to becoming a completely apostate and prodigal nation—one of the most ungodly nations—in the Last Days. Based on the trend analysis of our nation's trajectory away from God, the reasonable, logical and most likely conclusion is that America will be punished and destroyed by Almighty God for its disobedience and sins like every other superpower empire in history; and therefore, will no longer be a global superpower on the world's stage during the 7-year Tribulation period of the End Times that is prophesied in the Bible. This Tribulation period of the End Times is when God will complete His discipline of Israel (Daniel 9:24–27, 12:1, Jeremiah 30:4–7, Matthew 24:15–21), and finalize His judgment of the unbelieving world (Zephaniah 1:2–3, 14–18, Isaiah 2:12–21, 13:6–9, Joel 1:15, 2:1–3, 1 Thessalonians 5:1–3, Matthew 24:21–44,

Revelation 6:1–20:15). This statistical conclusion means unbelieving America will either have received its final judgment of destruction from God *before* the Tribulation period, creating a power vacuum of Israel's American safety net, or America will be included in God's final judgment of destruction of all the unbelieving nations in the world *during* the Tribulation period.

Still having a hard time envisioning God destroying America with the other nations during the End Times? Imagine an America where the Baby Boomers and Gen Xers lived out their lifespan and are all gone; and the only generations still alive are Millennials (only 12% Millennials believe in God), Gen Zers (the first post-Christian generation in America), and the following generations after them (more post-Christian than Gen Zers). What makes you think these remaining generations in America will side with a God they don't believe in instead of siding with the antichrist they can see during the End Times? The Bible tells us, *"They perish because they refused to love the truth and so be saved. For this reason God sends them a powerful delusion so that they will believe the lie and so that all will be condemned who have not believed the truth but have delighted in wickedness."* (2 Thessalonians 2:10–12 NIV)

It's time we pulled our spiritual heads out of Satan's sandpit of deception and see the writing on the wall from God. The Bible clearly states, *"That day will not come until there is a great rebellion against God and the man of lawlessness* [antichrist] *is revealed—the one who brings destruction."* (2 Thessalonians 2:3 NLT, bracketed emphasis mine) Other versions of the Bible translate those words "*a great rebellion*" against God as "*apostasy*" (BLB, NASB, CSB, and HCSB) and "*falling away*" (NKJV, KJB, JB 2000, and ASV). According to all the statistics and polls of America's growing decline in Christianity with each new generation, America's new generations will in all likelihood be a part of the great rebellion, falling away and apostasy against God in the End Times.

God has already started giving our nation glimpses of how quickly and easily His judgment can come upon our nation for our sins. With the growing proliferation of nuclear weapons, all it would take is a nuclear missile attack from a rogue nation such as North Korea, a nuclear first-strike from a nuclear powerful nation such as Russia, or the effects of a single terrorist nuclear bomb in the heart of a major US city to bring our nation to its knees for its sins—which is where our nation's knees need to be right now in prayer before this destruction happens. God is giving our nation the same type of "false alarms" of incoming death and destruction that Hawaii recently experienced to wake us up and realize that we are on the verge of total destruction; and we are *not ready* to meet our Maker.

Most Americans think America is still that Christian nation that is a "city on a hill" and a "light to other nations" instead of the increasingly sinful and prodigal nation that it now is. That's why so many people, including Christians, in our nation think it is incredulous to say God is punishing our nation for our sins. The reason we Christians find it hard to believe that God would punish America for our sins is because we Christians see ourselves as Americans first and Christians second. We Christians need to get our sight and insight back: we believers in America are Christians first and Americans second. When we Americans look at ourselves in the mirror, we still see that righteous, holy nation that has not turned its back on God—that's the deception Satan wants Americans to see. When we Christians look at America in the mirror of God's word, we should see a nation that is becoming more prodigal, more apostate, more sinful and more disobedient to God with each new generation. Every poll and statistic about the decline of Christianity in America bears that out.

Because of our blindness to the true spiritual condition of our nation, God's punishment of our nation will catch most people in America by surprise—as I was when pulling back that curtain in my dream. Our nation's destruction will surprise Americans the same way that gigantic wall of water took me by surprise; or when the Flood during Noah's day overtook the inhabitants of the earth by surprise; or when the destruction of Sodom and Gomorrah with fire and brimstone caught their people by surprise—they didn't even see it coming until it was too late. It was life and business as usual until their destruction hit them. Our Lord Jesus was also thinking of our nation when He said, *"Just as it happened in the days of Noah, so it will be also in the days* [Last Days] *of the Son of Man* [Jesus Christ]: *they were eating, they were drinking, they were marrying, they were being given in marriage, until the day that Noah entered the ark, and the flood came and destroyed them all. It was the same as happened in the days of Lot: they were eating, they were drinking, they were buying, they were selling, they were planting, they were building; but on the day that Lot went out from Sodom it rained fire and brimstone from heaven and destroyed them all. It will be just the same on the day that the Son of Man* [Jesus] *is revealed."* (Luke 17:26–30 NASB, bracketed emphasis mine)

But God in His mercy is listening to the prayers of those who are praying for our nation's revival and return back to Him; and for this reason, He is giving our nation more time to repent. God through His Holy Spirit is prompting me to pray and prompting you to pray for our nation. That's why God gave me these recurring dreams of a gigantic wall of water coming my way—He wanted me to get on my knees and pray for our nation because His patience is reaching its end for our nation; and He is now seriously considering the destruction of our nation for our sins. He's looking for people to stand in the gap and pray for revival.

God has entrusted America with the stewardship of His word—the Bible—and Christianity for Americans, and to keep our light of the Gospel of Christ burning brightly for all other nations in the world to see; but now we have buried that light under a bushel. The Apostle Paul said, *"It is required in stewards that one be found faithful."* (1 Corinthians 4:2 NKJV) We must remember the sobering words of our Lord Jesus who spoke of God's punishment of the unfaithful in the End Times this way: *"That servant who knew his master's will but did not get ready or do what his master asked will receive a severe beating. But the one who did not know his master's will and did things worthy of punishment will receive a light beating. From everyone who has been given much, much will be required, and from the one who has been entrusted with much, even more will be asked."* (Luke 12:47–48 NET) America is a nation to whom God has given much and entrusted much. We were a nation that knew its Master's will but we neither got our people ready for Christ's return nor did we do what our Master asked of us. Because of all the blessings God has given our nation, God expects more—not less— godliness, obedience and faith from our nation; therefore, our punishment will be *severe*, not a light beating.

Just because we appear to have dodged a nuclear bullet with the North Korea-United States summit between President Trump and Kim Jong-un, this doesn't mean God won't bring disaster upon our nation if we don't look into the mirror of God's word and change our ways. If we don't take God's warnings and wrath seriously and choose to continue in our rebellion and disobedience against Him, we too will suffer the same consequences as Sodom and Gomorrah, Nineveh and the Assyrians, the nations of Israel and Judah, the Babylonians, Medes and Persians, Greece, the Roman empire, and all other nations in history who turned their backs on God, both Jew and Gentile. History always repeats itself.

The Answer to America's Prodigal Spirit – Revival

Is there hope for America? So what's the answer to stopping America's spiraling death fall?

- Christians must get on their knees and cry out to God to have mercy upon our nation the way He had mercy on the nations of Israel and Judah when they cried out to Him; to spare our nation from destruction the way He spared Nineveh when they repented; to not destroy the righteous with the wicked in our nation the way He spared Lot and his family from the destruction of Sodom and Gomorrah at the request of Abraham.

- Christian ministers, Christian teachers, Christian churches and Christian ministries must be revived and re-awakened first before our nation can experience revival and a re-awakening. Revival never happened in a city or nation without God first reviving and re-awakening a Christian who would stand up and speak out about God's word boldly and truthfully—that word of God must include speaking boldly about the reality of God's *wrath* and the existence of *hell* along with God's love, grace and forgiveness in Christ.

- We Christians must pray for revival and the "Great Awakening" first to happen to <u>ALL</u> of our Christian ministers, Christian teachers, Christian churches and Christian ministries; and secondly, to pray for revival and the Great Awakening to happen for all Americans again. (2 Chronicles 7:14)

- Christianity in America must stop neglecting the teaching of God's *wrath* and *hell* and give our nation the straight truth about both God's goodness and *severity*. (Romans 11:22)

- America must wake up and realize we are a prodigal nation in the swine pit of sin; that we are no longer that city on a hill that shines brightly for Christ to other nations; that we are in a spiraling death fall because of our disobedience and sins against God; and we must humbly return to the Lord. (Luke 15:11–20)

- It's time America humbles itself before God again, prays to Him again, seeks His face again, and turns from our wicked ways again. Only then will God hear the prayers of our nation, forgive the sins of our nation and heal our nation. (2 Chronicles 7:14)

- Parents must once again teach their children about the Lord; taking them to church again where their children can learn about God; providing their children a good foundation of who God is and telling them the truth about His love and severity and power to ensure the next generation puts their faith in God.

"We will not hide these truths from our children; we will tell the next generation about the glorious deeds of the LORD, about His power and His mighty wonders. For He issued His laws to Jacob; He gave His instructions to Israel. He commanded our ancestors to teach them to their children, so the next generation might know them—even the children not yet born—and they in turn will teach their own children. So each generation should set its hope anew on God, not forgetting His glorious miracles and obeying His commands." (Psalm 78:4–7 NLT)

Only then will America come out of this nuclear nightmare ending of our nation—just like in my recurring dreams from God.

I, Jesus, have sent My angel to testify to you these things in the churches. I am the Root and the Offspring of David, the Bright and Morning Star. And the Spirit and the bride say, "Come!" And let him who hears say, "Come!" Let him who thirsts come. Whoever desires, let him take the water of life freely.

Revelation 22:16 NKJV

Straight from My Heart

You, Lord, are good, and ready to forgive, and abundant in mercy to all those who call upon You.

Psalm 86:5 NKJV

I wrote this book to give you help, wisdom, encouragement, hope and success in your search for God and in your Christian walk. It is my sincere hope that this book has blessed you, inspired you, strengthened you, and encouraged you in your faith.

I know what it's like falling, failing and being at the bottom in life; and I've learned that Jesus is there to catch your fall if you will only put your trust in Him. If you're not attending church, I encourage you to find a church in your local area. If you need help finding a church in your local area, pray this prayer with me:

> *Lord Jesus, I want to return back to Your house and Your people. Show me and lead me to the right church for me in my local area. Amen.*

If you've never put your trust in Christ, then invite Jesus into your heart and life by saying this simple prayer with me:

> *Lord Jesus, I acknowledge I am a sinner in need of a Savior. I repent of my sins. Forgive me of my sins, come into my life and give me Your Holy Spirit to live this life now and forever with You. Amen.*